Dr Ross Walker is an eminent cardiologist with a passion for people and health.

He graduated from the University of New South Wales with Honours in 1979 and became a Fellow of the Royal Australasian College of Physicians (FRACP) in 1986. His special interests are advanced echocardiology and preventative cardiology. He is the author of the best-selling books *If I Eat Another Carrot I'll Go Crazy*, *What's Cookin' Doc*, *Highway to Health* and *The Cell Factor*, all concentrating on lifestyle issues and in particular diet, antioxidants and health.

Dr Walker lectures extensively throughout the world to medical and business groups. He often discusses health and stress in the Australian media and has a weekly program on Radio 6PR in Perth and a monthly show on Radio 2CH in Sydney, in which he discusses preventative health issues.

He lives in Sydney and is married with five children.

THE LIFE FACTOR

DR ROSS WALKER

M.B., B.S. (HONS), F.R.A.C.P.

MACMILLAN

Pan Macmillan Australia

First published 2004 in Macmillan by Pan Macmillan Australia Pty Limited
St Martins Tower, 31 Market Street, Sydney

Reprinted 2004

National Library of Australia
Cataloguing-in-Publication data:

Walker, Ross G.T.
The life factor.

ISBN 1 40503573 0.

1. Stress (Psychology). 2. Self-actualization (Psychology).
I. Title.

155.9042

Papers used by Pan Macmillan Australia Pty Ltd are natural, recyclable
products made from wood grown in sustainable forests. The manufacturing
processes conform to the environmental regulations of the country of origin.

Set in 12/15 pt Fairfield by Seymour Designs
Printed in Australia by McPherson's Printing Group

To Jim and Mary

Contents

Unlocking the power of the Life Factor   1

PART I: The problem   7

Chapter 1   The origins of stress   9
Chapter 2   Energy: Are you drained?   22
Chapter 3   Fear: Who's afraid?   35
Chapter 4   Early days: Laying the foundations   59
Chapter 5   Am I stressed?   71

PART II: The Life Factor solution   89

Chapter 6   Goal-setting   91
Chapter 7   Out with the bad   111
Chapter 8   In with the good   149
Chapter 9   Which planet are you from?   166
Chapter 10   Think outside the square: Creative solutions   188

Further reading   218
Index   220

Unlocking the power of the Life Factor

How many of us can honestly say that we are truly happy with our lives? How many of us cope easily with day-to-day pressures? Are you content with your relationships and do you derive pleasure from most activities? If you can answer 'yes' to these questions, I would suggest that you are in the minority. So, why are so many people unhappy? Why do they find it so hard to cope and why are they discontented?

Despite extraordinary advances in technology that have led to enormous improvements in many of our creature comforts, it appears that our social world is continuing to deteriorate. We are witnessing unparalleled global terrorism, exposure of corruption at the highest levels in corporations, and the continuing existence of brutal regimes and their ongoing wars which reap carnage on innocent civilians. Despite the surface sophistication of many societies, primitive behaviour is rife.

As a species, humans are still in an early stage of evolution. For humans to truly develop, we need to adopt new ideas and strategies to cope with the inadequacies and contradictions that are funda-mental to the human condition. But, rather than using our inade-quacies as a positive impetus to improve our lives, things are going horribly awry. Where have we gone wrong and what can we do to resolve these dilemmas? *The Life Factor* explains the problem – and its solution. In the following chapters I will discuss the main reasons why modern society is so stressful. An important fact which is often downplayed by many experts in the field is that stress happens; it feels lousy when it happens but it can often be used as motivation for self-improvement.

I recently returned from a speaking engagement in Tahiti, one of the most beautiful places on earth. While I was there I had the pleasure of swimming on the private island once owned by the famous painter Paul Gauguin. But I asked myself the question: could I live there? Although I would be happy to visit on a rather frequent basis, I probably would be bored beyond belief were I to spend a prolonged sojourn in this paradise.

On my return to busy Sydney, I was confronted by the traffic jams and pollution of a crowded city and the expected stresses of the modern world. In many ways, though, these stresses contribute the necessary fuel to drive us towards seeking an improved situation and attitude.

I am in no way saying, 'Oh great – more stress.' But if we can harness this stress, learn from the experience and eventually turn it into a positive, we become stronger, wiser people.

This is what I mean when I talk about the Life Factor. The Life Factor is what we all crave. It is not money, it is not the acquisition of goods or some pill or potion to give us a temporary rush – it is peace and happiness. It is the ability to experience joy when many others would feel pain.

Life's journey will never be completely smooth and trouble-free. It is vital that we use all our life experiences – good and bad – as opportunities for growth. How many times have you heard of seemingly ordinary people who, despite extremely traumatic life experiences, work through these to enrich their lives and improve their situation? Equally, we hear of many people who use life traumas as an excuse for their current life situation or aberrant behaviour.

It is all about the decisions we make.

Carl and Brendan had a very traumatic childhood. Their father was a career criminal and longstanding heroin addict. Their mother tried her hardest to be a supportive parent, despite having to cope with bringing up the two boys by herself most of the time.

Carl excelled at school and was very successful at university, completing a law degree with honours and gaining a top position in a law firm. He was a supportive husband and a good father to his two young children.

Brendan, however, started experimenting with drugs in his early teens and by adulthood was using and dealing in heroin, cocaine and whatever else he could get his hands on. When Carl was asked what contributed to his success, his reply was, 'What else would you expect with the sort of childhood I had?'

When Brendan was asked why his life went off the rails, he gave exactly the same reply. Carl decided to react to his circumstances in a positive way; Brendan in a negative way.

When we realise the simple but important fact that each of us is the ultimate decision-maker in our life and not the victim of our circumstances, we are well on our way to unlocking the power of the Life Factor.

The well-known and controversial Australian radio and television personality Stan Zemanek emphatically states that there is no such thing as stress. For those who know Stan, it is unusual for him to have such a definite opinion!

So, does stress really exist? What is it?

Stress is defined in the dictionary as 'a great pressure or strain'. We even have a set of glands in the body known as the adrenal glands, which are mainly devoted to the production of stress hormones. I'm sorry, Stan – if stress doesn't exist, someone should tell the people who wrote the dictionary or better still the guy who designed the human body. In Stan's defence, I believe what he is inferring is that many people use the diagnosis of stress as an excuse for all sorts of problems and behaviours. Years ago, notions such as counselling, stress leave or Prozac were unheard of but these days they're terms that are in everyday use. I agree with Stan completely that as a society we're too quick to blame everything on stress and in many ways give people a way out of dealing with their problems. But, with the increasing complexity of modern society for all the reasons we have already discussed, our stress response is being switched on more and more.

So we can either allow ourselves to be ruined by stress, as was the case with Brendan, or react to stress in a proactive way, as Carl did, enriching our lives in the process.

But to understand our stress reactions, we must first examine the origins of stress. In chapter 1, I will discuss the automatic systems that drive our subconscious reactions to various life events. These systems began as survival mechanisms but in our modern world can work against our wellbeing in many situations.

Imperfections, inadequacies and contrasts are also a normal and important aspect of the human condition, and we can harness them, along with stress, to allow us to evolve as better people.

We cannot exist without energy and we need to aim for balance in the five aspects of our energy – physical, mental, emotional, sensual and spiritual. Neglecting any one of these areas contributes to ineffective stress coping mechanisms. Energy is discussed in chapter 2.

In chapter 3, I will introduce the five basic fears that often derail our ability to achieve the Life Factor.

Chapter 4 explores how our life passages contribute to the ways we deal with stress. Many of the stresses we experience as adults have their origins in our childhood experiences. In chapter 5, I discuss how you can identify if you're suffering from stress. Understanding the ways in which stress shows itself and recognising the early warning symptoms and signs are vital tools for stress management.

In Part 2 of the book I outline my five-step Life Factor solution, which involves the following important concepts.

Goal-setting: One of the major aspects of a fulfilling life is to know where you are going and what you are trying to achieve by arriving there. You can learn how to set goals that will crystallise your values and give your life purpose.

Bad and good coping mechanisms: With so many wonderful coping mechanisms available to us, why do we spend so much time chasing the bad ones? You can deal effectively with acute stress, rid yourself of your bad coping mechanisms – including addictions – and institute a program based around the good ones.

The occurrence of stress is, in many ways, a loss. Loss of control over a situation, loss of money, loss of a relationship, and so on. This loss can induce a grief reaction. I will explain how to turn this grief around, once you have worked through your initial 'stress response'.

Relationships: Your life is a series of ongoing relationships that occur on many levels. You can improve and maintain a balance in your relationships that will in turn create lasting fulfilment in your life.

Creative solutions: So much of our day is spent in automatic pilot mode. Thinking differently about how you manage your life from moment to moment can lead to major positive changes in your life.

It is not particularly difficult to find the money to purchase a book, such as this one, that claims to be life-changing. It is not much more of an effort to read the book. The hard part comes when you have to put the concepts in this book into action. Throughout *The Life Factor*, I will give you specific action plans to make this hardest step easy and achievable.

So now that we've established that stress is a true entity, one we ignore at our peril, I will end this introduction on a positive note. Although the world is changing (at times for the worse), I am still witnessing positive changes on many levels. People are becoming more aware and certainly less accepting of corruption and inequality, whether at a personal, institutional or national level. Recent history has seen the demise of apartheid and of many brutal communist regimes. We have seen dictators forced from power. Big business and multinational corporations are being held more accountable for their actions and policies.

At a personal level, the rights of disadvantaged and disabled people have improved. The horror of child abuse has been high-lighted and harsher punishments for offenders are being intro-duced.

People are also increasing their spiritual awareness. Harsh, crass materialism can often distract us from spiritual goals. But higher values such as truth, integrity and honesty are not being lost and still hold an important place in the world.

If you feel unhappy and stressed-out, you're missing so much of what life has to offer. I truly believe that my five-point solution will provide you with the strategies to move towards achieving the Life Factor for yourself – not just for a fleeting moment but permanently.

PART I

The
PROBLEM

CHAPTER 1

The origins of stress

'We cannot solve our current problems with the same thinking we used to create them' – Albert Einstein

It is defective thinking along with defective perceptions of our problems that have created our current dilemmas, both at a macrocosmic and microcosmic level. The world is deluged with political, social and economic conflicts but additionally many individuals are afflicted with numerous external and internal conflicts.

DECISION AND AWARENESS

I will refer throughout this book to two important basic concepts, both central to dealing with these conflicts: decision and awareness. It is your choice whether your life experiences plunge you deeper into despair or become part of the motivation that drives you towards change for the better.

I am always amused when I hear someone say, 'That person is the most irritating person I have ever met!' What this person is actually saying is, 'I have made the subconscious decision to allow that person to irritate me!'

It is your decision how you react to your experiences, and your decision can determine future benefit or harm in your life. A decision to turn a negative experience into a positive can alter the path of your life permanently. You can choose to be dragged along in 'the wake of the boat' or to be the person in control of your life's direction.

The only certainty of life on our planet is that all living things have a beginning and an end. Thus, individually, each one of us has a major design fault: our mortality. Eventually our imperfect system will fail, making way for newer bipedal carbon-based life forms to take our place.

Not only is ours a world of imperfection, it is also a world of contrasts. Without evil, there would be no good. Without black, no white. Without boredom, there are no peak experiences.

Our world of imperfection and contrasts, however, allows us to fully experience life. Perhaps up until now your life experience has not been so great, but that doesn't have to be the case. With the Life Factor approach you can move beyond your present dilemmas to a new and empowering attitude that will change the way you think and experience, permanently.

As we are all imperfect, we all have a sense of inadequacy. Although feelings of inadequacy can manifest in many negative ways, there is also a positive slant. It is my belief that feelings of inadequacy are the major driver of the human spirit. I believe that there is potential in every human being to improve as they travel along life's fascinating journey. We develop the desire to improve because of our feelings of inadequacy – and we have feelings of inadequacy because we are imperfect.

Life also presents us with other human beings who, for whatever reason, appear more adequate than us. Thus, imperfections and contrasts drive our sense of inadequacy which in turn drives our desire to improve. If we were to collectively realise this simple fact, the world would be ever improving as time marches on.

The second major concept of the Life Factor is awareness. An ongoing dilemma for philosophers, psychologists, neuroscientists and other health professionals is the question of what constitutes the 'real' you. Are you a mind, body and spirit living in the physical world or is your reality constituted by a bunch of biochemical–metabolic reactions?

Are 'you' the doer or the observer of the doing? Our awareness or consciousness of our own actions and existence in many ways constitutes who we are. Regardless of the metaphysical responses to these big questions, no-one can be really 100 per cent certain, whilst living, that they have the answer.

However, many people agree that plunging into awareness mode enhances the quality of your decisions and thus the quality of your life. If we do not diligently train and maintain our awareness of our day-to-day behaviour and reactions to life events, we rapidly slip back into our ingrained default mechanisms. These are based on character and personality traits and developed through years of life experiences and, at times, distorted belief systems and opinions.

Persistent succumbing to our default mechanisms stunts our growth as human beings and reinforces behavioural patterns that often serve us poorly. Awareness of our behaviour, positioning ourselves as observers of our actions and situation, rather than as just the 'doers', allows us to monitor and change unsatisfactory aspects of our lives.

How many times have you said to yourself, why did I say that? Why did I 'fly off the handle' over a trivial incident? Being self-aware and able to monitor yourself in such situations allows you to correct this unwanted habit.

So, I am suggesting that it is a vital part of the Life Factor approach to consciously train yourself to be aware. Every chance you get, slip into the observer mode. Be alert to high-risk situations that may precipitate your default behaviour or reaction. These situations will immediately trigger you into awareness and in the process prevent your old default mechanism from switching into gear.

The human brain is the most sophisticated piece of machinery known. This particular piece of hardware has not only created works of art, architecture, music and all manner of astounding technologies, it has been and unfortunately will continue to be responsible for all manner of depravity, destruction, despair and suffering.

In many ways, we are in control of this fascinating organ (although we are yet to discover who the real 'we' is – maybe it's just the brain itself). Every second of the day and night your brain is registering multiple bits of information to ensure the smooth functioning of the entire organism.

There are two major systems that deserve mention. These systems are responsible for your own particular reactions to the many stresses that will come your way on a day-to-day basis. They are:

▶ the automatic (autonomic) nervous system
▶ the pleasure–reward–motivation system.

THE AUTONOMIC NERVOUS SYSTEM

When man and woman first squirmed their way out of the primordial soup to assume their position at the top of the food chain, many aspects of existence were about avoiding danger.

Being at the top of the food chain did not afford you an instant guarantee against attack from those below you or, in fact, from those who shared the numero uno position. Thus, ancient Homo sapiens were always on guard against attacks from sabre-toothed tigers and even neighbouring tribes who might act in a decidedly 'unneighbourly' fashion. Without his autonomic nervous system, Mr Homo sapiens would have been in big trouble.

The autonomic nervous system is divided into two opposing systems:

> ▸ the sympathetic (fear–flight/fight) system
> ▸ the parasympathetic (relaxation/rejuvenation) system.

THE SYMPATHETIC NERVOUS SYSTEM

Let's see how this system works by looking at a hypothetical. Say you have never given a presentation to a large audience before. One week ago, your boss informed you that he was urgently called overseas and needed you to give a presentation to the entire sales force on a topic you are an expert in, but have not spoken about in front of an audience.

It is now five minutes before the designated time for your speech. The current speaker is rambling on and you are starting to feel nervous. Your palms are sweaty, your heart is thumping rapidly and you have an uncomfortable fullness in your head. Yes, your sympathetic nervous system – the old fear–flight/fight system is in action. You try to calm yourself down, but each time you look at the lectern and the size of the crowd you're speaking to, it clicks back into overdrive.

Why do we have this system at all? Why do we have to suffer these uncontrollable symptoms in times of terror?

The reason goes back to the old 'sabre-toothed tiger' days. Without the sympathetic nervous system, if we were presented with a life-threatening situation, events would go something like this: 'Oh no, I'm about to be attacked by a sabre-toothed tiger! I'd better get the blood flowing to my muscles as quickly as I can so that I can start running.'

As the heart slowly starts clicking into gear, you eventually deliver enough blood to give those muscles their very much needed oxygen supply.

By the time your muscles are ready for action, the sabre-toothed tiger has already finished his main course (that is, the tastiest portion of your slowly mobilising body).

I think you can probably see my point. The sympathetic nervous system gets you ready rapidly. It's therefore protection – a very important survival mechanism.

If you are in sudden danger, the sympathetic nervous system, through a series of rapid-fire nervous impulses including the release of adrenaline and noradrenaline, cranks up your system immediately so blood is directed away from the abdominal organs, increasing by a factor of five the blood flow to your brain and muscles and increasing your awareness, acuity and muscle strength. This gives you the best chance of effectively dealing with any particular acute danger with which you may be presented.

On the downside, this same system is activated during the more modern situations of terror such as public speaking, a meeting with an angry boss or co-worker, or the numerous traumatic incidents related to negotiating modern-day hazards such as traffic accidents, road rage or that little piece of equipment known as the radar trap. Ah well, no system is perfect!

THE PARASYMPATHETIC NERVOUS SYSTEM

The last thing you need when your body descends into phase 4 non-REM sleep, whilst the system is trying to rejuvenate itself, is a heart that is pumping at maximum speed and volume, giving torrential blood flow to your muscles.

Enter the opposing system, the parasympathetic nervous system. The parasympathetic nervous system winds your metabolism down to minimal activity. Deep sleep, meditation or some other form of relaxation automatically switches on the parasympathetic nervous system. This rejuvenation is also essential for survival. Without it, we cannot replenish our reserves for more active times.

Both the sympathetic and the parasympathetic nervous system – the two components of our autonomic nervous system – have been carefully designed for our survival. The secret is in learning how to utilise both these systems in a balanced way and not allowing imbalance to drive the sympathetic nervous system so that it becomes a dominant factor in your life.

THE PLEASURE–REWARD–MOTIVATION SYSTEM

Our basic needs for food, shelter, socialising and procreation are also a survival mechanism. Many of our activities, from ancient times to the modern world, have been geared towards the acquisition and maintenance of these basic needs.

As we actively seek to fulfil these needs, we put into operation the pleasure–reward–motivation system to make the associated activities pleasurable.

Ancient man is often referred to as a hunter–gatherer, obviously due to his methods of acquiring food. Ancient man is also called a 'caveman' in reference to his particular choice of shelter. Being a member of a tribe and family points to the socialisation and procreative abilities of the species.

These activities continue (rightly so) to play a key role in all societies because without them the individual, and collectively the tribe, will not survive.

Whereas the autonomic nervous system is operated by the neurotransmitters adrenaline and noradrenaline for the sympathetic nervous system and acetylcholine for the parasympathetic nervous system, the pleasure–reward–motivation system uses the chemical dopamine for the 'desire and anticipation' aspect of seeking food, shelter, socialisation and that enjoyable activity that leads to procreation.

Another aspect of the pleasure–reward–motivation system uses a different set of neurotransmitters, our body's natural opiates – known as endorphins – to give us that feeling of 'dreamy satisfaction' once our desire has been achieved.

In a natural, chemical-free world, the autonomic nervous system and the pleasure–reward–motivation system would both be very effective in affording us protection against danger, rejuvenating our bodies during relaxation and sleep and maintaining our motivation to seek our basic needs.

But we live in more 'sophisticated' societies!

Ever since we have had the opportunity, we have searched for ways to overstimulate both these systems. Unfortunately, many of these artificial techniques have very significant downsides. The 'adrenaline junkies', who seek all manner of novel experiences that would strike terror in the hearts of most of us, often end up with some nasty consequence of their behaviour.

From the conventional thrill-seeking activities such as Formula One racing or jumping out of planes (usually with a parachute!) to the more bizarre acts such as base-diving off large cliffs or wrestling crocodiles, the list goes on. All adrenaline-inducing behaviours have a common substrate – they are dangerous.

Hyperstimulation of the pleasure–reward–motivation system has other downsides. Some people constantly activate this system by seeking novel relationships (at the expense of longstanding established relationships), usually with disastrous consequences. And there is the even more serious issue of the total hijacking of this system by means of an addiction. Any pharmacological addiction induces hyperstimulation, either by dopamine secretion in particular parts of the brain or directly via opiates such as heroin or morphine.

Once normal mechanisms have been hijacked, it becomes very difficult to function normally. Thus, once an individual becomes an addict, they begin a process of degradation in their life. They tend to spend most of their time in activities geared towards seeking the object of their addiction and then satisfying their craving. Not only have they hijacked their pleasure–reward–motivation system, they have derailed their entire life.

I will discuss in chapter 7 the five-point method for beating addictions. Suffice to say now, however, that the best method for dealing with an addiction is to avoid it in the first place. Choose your poison carefully because if you don't, you will certainly suffer the consequences.

WHY ARE WE BECOMING MORE STRESSED?

Despite enormous advances in technology that have improved life in many ways, most people appear more stressed nowadays than they were years ago. Why is this so?

It is my view that over the past twenty years, society has undergone a radical change, creating a set of circumstances not seen in the preceding millennia of the civilised world. I believe there are five major contributors to our modern society's increasing stress response:

1 overabundance of choice
2 requirement for instant answers
3 need for multi-skilling
4 pace of change
5 increase in conflict situations, such as litigation.

1 OVERABUNDANCE OF CHOICE

Although choice allows a wide variety of experiences, it also has a major downside. The more choice, the more anxiety over those choices. Take, for example, all the extra functions on all manner of electronic goods. It is not difficult to understand how this plethora of choice can create enormous anxiety and stress.

Try programming a video or DVD player. You need a PhD in electronics to figure out how to set the date! Depending on the type of car you wish to purchase, there are probably around twenty choices in each car category. Processing these choices in your brain certainly can create an unwanted stress response.

Accompanying these extra categories of choice are extra considerations and options. Try ringing a company these days to speak to someone about a specific issue. You ring the number and an electronically recorded message allows you a series of numbered options, each with details that may loosely fit the issue you are calling about.

You need to make an instant choice and then probably push a few more buttons until you arrive at the inevitable message, 'Our operators are busy at the moment but your call is important to us . . .' What they don't say is that they expect you to listen to irritating music for the next 20 to 30 minutes, after which time one of their stressed-out operators will eventually tell you that you've reached the wrong department and they'll transfer you to someone who may or may not be able to help you – and by the way, please enjoy the next twenty minutes of muzak intermingled with the irritating reminder of how important your call is to the company.

No doubt you are beginning to agree that these many and varied choices are not always to our advantage.

2 REQUIREMENT FOR INSTANT ANSWERS

The telephone story illustrates another source of stress in modern life. We can no longer take time to contemplate our actions. Whilst enduring these tedious and prolonged phone calls, if you just happen to push the wrong button – it's curtains, baby! It's time to start all over again, hoping desperately that your brain registers every possible nuance and that you don't make any more foolish mistakes.

In our current world of instant communication via mobile phones, text messages, emails and fax machines, many people are communicating and in conflict at any time of the day or night, expecting instant answers to often poorly thought-out questions.

This increasingly urgent need for instant answers has undermined the vital importance of the practice of quiet contemplation for our physical, emotional, mental and spiritual wellbeing. As the famous French scientist Blaise Pascal once said, 'One of Man's greatest problems is his inability to sit quietly alone.'

Contemplation and reflection bring focus. Focus heightens awareness, which I have already mentioned is a major factor in dealing with stress.

When enormous demands are made on you to spit out instant answers, your stress response immediately switches on. Science has demonstrated time and time again in numerous psychological studies that a very effective way to induce the stress response is to ask a subject to perform rapid mental arithmetic – an effective analogy for any situation that demands instant answers.

A simple but sensible universal rule is: the quicker the answer, the greater the likelihood of it being wrong!

3 NEED FOR MULTI-SKILLING

Most people living in modern society need to develop multiple skills. The recent rise of emails as a major form of communication has forced most of us to learn basic word-processing skills. The value-added nature of businesses now dictates that they should offer more than their core services. Carwashes, bookstores and petrol stations no longer just offer their basic products. They are often cafes, supermarkets or even bakeries.

Multi-skilling places more demands and expectations on you and this is a recipe for more stress.

4 PACE OF CHANGE

Since September 11, the Bali bombings and numerous other terrorist attacks throughout the planet, our perception of the world has changed.

Mind you, the world has always been a violent place. But, as international travel becomes easier and quicker and global television networks keep us up to date with world conflicts, the nature and effects of this violence and change are much more at the forefront of our minds.

There is no doubt that dealing with constant change also promotes the stress response. We all enjoy our security and familiar habits and places. One of the greatest threats to this security is change.

5 LITIGATION AND OTHER CONFLICT SITUATIONS

Poor old lawyers really cop a pounding. Many would argue they deserve it. Whether they do or not (and I'll leave that up to you), the reality is that we are now living in a litigious world. In my field, medicine, the cost of medical defence has now climbed to ridiculous levels. Many doctors can no longer afford medical defence fees and some retire prematurely over such matters. Most doctors have been sued or have had threats of legal action, often justified, often not. With this increasing trend towards court action, the major winners are the lawyers, I can assure you.

But let's not just pick on the legal system. One increasingly common conflict situation, especially in Western societies, involves that wonderful invention called the motor vehicle. We humans are prone to making mistakes (well, we are only human). These days, if you make a mistake while driving there is a distinct possibility that you'll become a victim of road rage. So not only do you feel stressed about the possibility of causing an accident, you may also be dealing with a lunatic sounding their horn, screeching obscenities or threatening physical violence, just because you inadvertently changed lanes at the wrong time or because you slowed them down for some reason.

Another growing area of conflict, at a day to day level, is the burgeoning bureaucracy of most government and corporate bodies, and the increasing inflexibility created by their systems. One of my wife's pet hates is the concept of the 'primary card holder'. For some reason I seem to have been crowned 'primary card holder' in our household. The problem with this is that I am hardly ever available if there is an issue relating to the card that needs to be dealt with. When my wife rings an organisation to change our address or even arrange a simple transaction, she is often informed (usually after waiting the obligatory ten to twenty minutes before being connected to an operator) that she is not the 'primary card holder' and therefore under the privacy act she cannot be given such privileged information.

It's no wonder our stress levels are going through the roof!

YOU CAN HARNESS STRESS

The above five factors have been major contributors towards the epidemic of stress sweeping modern society. Rather than allowing these factors to defeat us, we should learn the strategies that will allow us to use stressful situations as motivation to drive us towards self-improvement. In Part II of *The Life Factor*, we'll explore these strategies.

CHAPTER 2

Energy: Are you drained?

In every aspect of our lives we are totally dependent on energy. Simply stated, the existence of life on our planet is dependent on the energy we obtain from the many types of light emanating from the sun. The subsequent growth of vegetation and production of oxygen fuels the essential chemicals that drive our cells, allowing them to perform their many necessary functions. We derive energy from the food we eat. This food provides us with the basic nutrients that work in concert with oxygen to maintain our cellular function.

But energy takes many forms and, in many circumstances, it is very difficult to measure. How many times have you heard someone say, 'I just can't understand where he gets so much energy'?

Such comments are really focusing on the fact that some people have the energy or ability to perform the myriad activities and functions of their life, whereas others appear to have no energy and find it hard to even drag themselves out of bed in the morning.

So what is energy? Energy is the basic unit of power which is really the sum total of all aspects of our being. It is the internal force that allows us to be proactive and to contribute or, if we lack energy, to be negative and inactive. So how do we achieve the energy that allows us to make this important contribution to life, not only at a cellular and individual level but also to the people we love, to those in our immediate environment, to those in our community and also on a global basis? I believe every individual has the potential to tap into this great source of universal energy and make important contributions at every level.

FIVE KINDS OF ENERGY

In order to understand and fully utilise our energy, I believe we should examine the way it functions in each aspect of our being. I have identified five kinds of energy, each of which is essential for our continuing wellbeing. They are our physical, mental, emotional, sensual and spiritual energies.

PHYSICAL ENERGY

Let's start with the most basic form of energy – physical energy. Physical energy allows us to perform our normal daily functions. The amount of physical energy we have is directly related to oxygen supply, nutrition, physical fitness, life expectations and the amount of stress we are suffering. Dividing a typical day into periods of work, leisure and sleep, I believe that an average healthy person without any obvious physical diseases would have enough energy stores in their body for around eight hours of solid work, eight hours for leisure and eight hours for sleep. Obviously, this is simplistic and is extremely variable depending on each person's individual metabolism and life – but what the heck, it's a neat generalisation.

Someone who is malnourished, or does not get enough sleep or, most significantly, has some form of physical disease, will not be able to efficiently obtain fuel from their cells to give them this energy.

The function of sleep is to rejuvenate you for the next day. We derive most of this rejuvenation from very deep sleep. You know the kind of sleep I'm talking about; it's the kind where to wake someone up you have to shake them for about three to five minutes, pour cold water over their head or if you're into torture, you could even start playing Barry Manilow music (only kidding, in fact, I must admit I quite enjoy 'Copacabana').

If you suffer from heart disease, cancer or some other chronic illness, your body cannot generate enough energy to keep you going for the day. You therefore might only manage two hours of solid work energy and six to seven hours of relaxation before having to go to sleep to regain some lost energy fuel. The only way around this is to obtain adequate sleep, adequate nutrition or effectively manage the underlying disease process, if you have one.

It really gets back to having a physical balance in your life and the Life Factor is all about achieving that balance. Creating balance in your physical energy comes from having or establishing in your life the principles I have firmly stated in my previous books – the five-point way to a healthy life through:

1 proper nutrition
2 adequate exercise and movement
3 no smoking
4 sensible or no alcohol consumption
5 an ongoing stress management plan.

MENTAL ENERGY

The next aspect of energy that I want to examine is mental energy, which we need for all aspects of our mental processes. We need it for adequate conversation; for listening; to perform simple tasks; and for complex tasks. It is the energy we need for dealing with problems at work and at home. To some extent, our mental energy is dependent on biochemical processes but we maintain the chemistry of our brain through its adequate use and stimulation. We use it or lose it.

You often hear people say, 'I'm only doing this course so I can become X and perform job Y.' It is not often that you hear people say, 'I'm going to do this course because I love learning.' We should see every piece of reading, conversation or any form of knowledge acquisition as an end in itself. Every time we have to use mental processes to solve a problem and learn a new piece of information, we are keeping those mental processes in good working order. Interestingly, we can wear out our material goods and even our bodies through careless overuse and abuse. But the more we maintain our bodies and the more we maintain our brain, the more developed, aware and astute it becomes. As has often been said, most people only use 5 per cent of their true brain potential. The more you attempt to improve this figure, the smarter you will become. It's commonly assumed that as we get older, our brains generally become less efficient – and if we accept this assumption it will certainly happen. If we begin to expect that we will slow down, inevitably we will slow down.

A dear friend of mine once told me how his father was lamenting at the age of 80 that his brain was not as sharp as it used to be. He then decided to commence a pure maths course at university. Within six months, he was back to his old self and, in fact, became much sharper than he had been for many years. The way to maintain and improve your mental energy is to use the organ that gives it to you in the first place. Never stop learning and broadening avenues in your life; never stop reading, especially challenging yourself with great works of literature or the biographies of great achievers.

NERVE CELLS AND NEUROTRANSMITTERS

Every reaction in the brain is dependent on the basic unit of brain function, which is the nerve cell. If I take my index finger and touch you on the back of your hand while your eyes are closed, you will perceive my touch. You'll be able to pinpoint, within 2–3 mm, exactly where I touched you and tell me whether it was a pleasurable or neutral sensation. If I then take a pin and prick you in exactly the same spot, you will immediately pull your hand away, indicate that the sensation was painful and possibly try to strangle me for doing it in the first place. But why did the first sensation feel neutral and the other one painful, despite the fact that both occurred in exactly the same place? The answer is, the guy who designed us knew we would need a system that not only would allow us to feel normal day-to-day events and interactions but also would protect us.

We can't go around experiencing the same reaction to normal stimuli as to painful stimuli, because then we would puncture our skin against sharp objects or burn our skin against hot objects. Within a few years of this ridiculous behaviour, our bodies would be mutilated.

How does this protective mechanism work? Different nerves have different chemicals running along them for different stimuli. These stimuli are also experienced in different parts of our brain. It takes longer for a normal stimulus to be registered in our brain than it does for a painful stimulus. So we can react much more quickly to a painful stimulus and thus protect ourselves. Those few milliseconds can mean the difference between moving our hand quickly from a hot object or developing a very nasty burn and having to spend quite a bit of time having it dressed at the emergency department.

So what drives these nerves to know the difference? The nerves are of the same basic structure, although some are a little thicker or thinner than others. The real driver is a group of substances known as neurotransmitters.

If you lead a life that is constantly stressful and you find it all too traumatic, you stimulate a whole different group of neurotransmitters than if you lead a deeply stimulating life but have a relaxed, peaceful and contented attitude. If, on the other hand, you live a boring and dull life, there are other chemicals, also neurotransmitters, that are released.

Even with an active fulfilled life, you still cannot expect to maintain energy levels and perform efficiently if you work sixteen hours a day and only have four hours' sleep. Again, it is all about balance. You need balance in your mental energy just as much as you need balance in your physical energy.

EMOTIONAL ENERGY

The third aspect of being is your emotions. Emotional energy is linked to mental energy but to an extent it involves different parts of the brain and also different neurotransmitters. Your emotional energy isn't just a function of the activity of brain chemicals. It is driven by another force – one which I believe is the ultimate energy – but more of that shortly.

There is no point living life almost like an automaton, attending to your physical and mental fulfilment by maintaining those energies but ignoring your emotional side. Probably one of the most fulfilling aspects of life is the maintenance of our emotional energy. Think of the feeling of unconditional love that develops after many years of a fulfilling, loving relationship with your spouse or partner or the amazing magical feeling of tenderness and love you have for your children. The love that my wife has given and continues to give me over the years is one of the most sustaining forces in my life. Without her support and inspiration, I would not have had the energy to be in the position I'm in today. My relationship with her is like an ongoing source of power. If I have had a hard day or have been upset or stressed by a particular problem, her calming influence and advice always restore my balance.

I cannot stress this enough: we are going 'off the rails' in our society when we forget the importance of emotional energy in our lives. By spending so much time furthering our careers and building up a strong financial base, we can lose sight of the most important aspects of life: our family and very close friends.

I know if I stopped my career tomorrow, I would probably be missed by a number of my patients and hopefully by my work colleagues – but if I left home or died, my family would be devastated.

I was talking to a good friend of mine recently. She related the story of her son, who at the age of fifteen developed testicular cancer. He went through agonising months of surgery and chemotherapy, but the love and support from his parents and family and most importantly his own personal strength helped him through an agonising ordeal. His amazing spirit and determination was such that he was invited to be involved in programs that helped others deal with the many problems associated with cancer. Over the years, he was a great support for many children with cancer.

Then his life turned around. His father decided that he wanted to start a new life with another woman, in the process devastating his children. His son, who had shown so much spirit in his fight against cancer, could not fight the emotional trauma of his parents splitting up. His entire attitude to life changed. He is now living in a drug commune in Holland and is a regular marijuana smoker, his spirit being broken.

What broke his spirit? I believe it was the loss of the emotional energy derived from believing that his parents had a solid relationship. As far as he saw it, his father had failed him; his emotional energy had been sapped.

One of the problems of turning to drugs as a cure for emotional pain is the long-term effect of these substances. Marijuana, especially, takes away your motivation and in some cases may slowly induce a dementing illness comparable to Alzheimer's disease in its effects. Therefore a person's insight into their own position is greatly reduced and it becomes much harder for them to drag themselves out of the situation they have created.

It is therefore so important for all of us to nurture our emotional energy. We can do this by nurturing relationships with the special people around us. When my daughters were younger, one of my greatest joys every day was to come home from a long day in my clinic to see my two beautiful little girls jump up and excitedly rush to greet me. There are not many other life experiences that can come close to this one.

SENSUAL ENERGY

The fourth aspect of our energy is sensual energy. I'm not just talking about sexual energy, although that is certainly one of my favourites. I am talking about the total approach; stimulating all the five senses: vision, taste, hearing, smell and touch. The old cliché about stopping and smelling the roses is actually sound advice and important if you are to maintain your total being. There is so much beauty in the world that is ignored every day.

I have a friend who is a paediatrician in a country town and although he has a brilliant mind he is not your typical obsessive, ordered doctor who never stops working. Every day as I drove to work I would see him take a detour to drive past the lookout. I stopped him one day and said, 'Why do you take the long way to work?' and he said, 'I love looking at the view every morning.'

A simple act that only took an extra minute or so in the morning certainly added to this man's quality of life and helped sustain his sensual energy in order to cope with a busy and at times very stressful job.

Your five senses can be stimulated in so many ways. The most obvious is the sensation of sight. Enjoy the beauty that is all around us in nature. How often do you stop and look at the structure of trees and other vegetation? Take any chance you have to look at a lovely natural scene. My wife and I once visited the Grand Canyon in Arizona. As we gazed at this awesome natural wonder, we were rewarded with a breathtaking experience which will stay with us forever.

Man-made structures have their own beauty. I once had the pleasure and privilege of travelling to Germany to learn a new cardiac technique. North from Bonn, where I was doing my training, is the city of Cologne. In this city, the tallest building is the cathedral built hundreds of years ago. It was the only major structure in Cologne not to be destroyed in World War II. To stand in front of this building and gaze at its magnificence was a truly awe-inspiring experience. A great way to improve one's sensual energy!

What about the sensation of smell? Smells can be amazingly beautiful or absolutely disgusting. They can have subtle but powerful effects, as demonstrated by our reactions to pheromones. Pheromones are substances secreted by the body in small amounts. They can either attract or repel other people or animals.

I would suggest that you take every opportunity to literally 'smell the roses' and other uplifting scents. Take notice of your partner's perfume or the wonderful fresh smell of the spring garden.

Stimulation of your auditory sensation can give you enormous energy. There are not too many people in the world who don't enjoy listening to some form of music. If you are not inspired by Beethoven's Sixth (Pastoral) Symphony or most of the works of the greatest musical genius who has ever lived (Mozart), perhaps you drive your car with the sound of the Beatles at full blast, or BB King, jazz or – for those of you with extremely bizarre tastes – country and western music. The choice is individual, but the stimulation provided by music is universal. There is sure to be some sort of music that excites your sensual energy.

Listen to an inspiring speaker presenting a lecture. Not just the content of the words but the sound of his or her voice, the intensity and passion with which they speak, can also have enormous benefits.

What about the sounds of nature? The early morning call of a kookaburra, the enormously rousing sound of thunder or the rustle of wind blowing through the trees. The list of wonderful and exciting sounds goes on; their significance lies in how you allow them to affect you.

What about the sensation of taste? It can be as varied as the savouring of a delicious meal, the taste of salt whilst swimming in the ocean or the taste of your lover's lips after a long passionate kiss.

It is interesting to note that when we eat different types of tasty food, it is really only the first ten to fifteen bites that have a profound effect on our taste buds. The real joy of eating comes from these first bites and the combination of different flavours in foods.

Why is it then that we have developed such an obsession in our society with gluttony? The epidemic of the 'all-you-can-eat' salad bars and 'bottomless' cups of coffee appeals to this disgusting sense of consumerism that is one of the factors eating away at our society. We need to get back to the necessary reasons for eating. You do not have to fill yourself to bursting point when you eat. Why don't you try eating without finishing everything on your plate? We derive enormous pleasure from eating, but the consequences of gluttony are disastrous.

Finally, the sensation of touch can be one of the most appropriate or inappropriate ways of transferring energy, depending on its context. In a negative sense, how many times have you felt invaded by people touching you even if it seems somewhat innocent? The so-called 'lounge lizard' at a party is all over every woman he sees. We often hear comments like, 'He could not keep his hands off me', or hear of the even more disturbing touch that unfortunately has become all too common in our society – child abuse.

Of course, all of these negative aspects of touching should not denigrate the wonderful and sensual aspects of touch. Positive, welcome touch can only enrich our lives and give us enormous energy.

I remember early in my medical career we were taught that a doctor should never touch a patient unless he or she is examining them. I have come to realise that this is just not true. Heartfelt emotions can be expressed from a warm handshake or a gentle touch on the shoulder just to show someone you care.

A few years back I practised cardiology in Coffs Harbour, New South Wales. Coffs Harbour is a small Australian coastal city of around 80,000 people. When I left Coffs Harbour, I had built up a loyal and wonderful clientele.

One of my most special patients was an absolutely beautiful lady in her late eighties. We had developed a close relationship over the years after I had salvaged her from cardiac arrest a few years before. When I told Alison, my 88-year-old patient, that sadly I was moving on, she broke down in tears and gave me an enormous warm hug, telling me she didn't know what she would do if I left. On the one hand the intensity of her emotions touched me with enormous sadness but on the other hand I also experienced enormous joy when thinking how privileged I had been to become so close to such a wonderful person. Often, so much more is said through touch than can be said in words.

Another wonderful form of touch is massage. You can derive enormous energy from any form of massage. I have been having a remedial massage on average once a fortnight for the last fifteen years. Not only does it keep my muscles in tune and stop the inevitable aches and pains, it also improves my energy levels. It is a wonderful stress relief. Massage was in the past often associated with the sex industry, but now remedial massage is well established as an extremely important therapeutic practice.

On an individual level, touch is an extremely important aspect of your personal relationships. There is nothing more therapeutic for a small child than the warmth of their mother's or father's hugs. Children always love being kissed good night and parents love the special touch of their children's cuddles.

Finally, there is nothing more sustaining than the loving touch between partners. It is very difficult to maintain any sort of reasonable relationship with a lover if you don't touch them, whether it be the simple innocence of holding hands or the deep caressing touch of lovemaking. All these aspects of touch are vitally important in maintaining your sensual energy.

SPIRITUAL ENERGY

Finally, in our quest to maintain energy we should not overlook spiritual energy. I'm not referring to any particular religion; I believe religion is a very personal and private matter. When I refer to spirituality, I'm talking about just that: your spirit.

As mentioned in chapter 1, the question of whether we are beings operated via neural pathways connecting our brain to all organs and parts of our body, or whether there is a spiritual aspect to our existence has plagued philosophers from Plato to Descartes and beyond. Once the oxygen supply is permanently cut off to our organs, once the organism dies, is that the end of the story? A rather damned depressing concept, if you ask me.

An alternative view is that either at conception or somewhere along the way, maybe in uterine development, the soul or spirit enters the body and resides there until death. One of the basic themes or arguments of religion is that during our time on earth, whether this is only a few short years or the usual life span of 70 to 80 years, we develop our spirit or soul through our life's experiences.

Some people have lives of great joy and fulfilment whereas others seem to go from one misery to the next. The real issue is not what your life situation is, but how you consciously or subconsciously decide to react to that situation. Viktor Frankl, in his classic work, *Man's Search for Meaning*, discusses these issues in great depth. Viktor Frankl spent quite a few years in a Nazi concentration camp and during his time in this camp, he observed that no matter what the degree of suffering a person endured, it was the way he responded to the suffering that determined his survival. Frankl was tortured by the Nazis but maintained his mighty spirit by realising that his freedom to decide how he dealt with that suffering could not be taken from him. This is, in fact, what is said to separate us from all other species on earth – our ability to think through abstract problems and make conscious decisions. We are in control of every emotion we experience.

The most fundamental aspect of our life is how we nurture our spiritual energy and growth. The most highly developed spirits on this earth exhibit an immense amount of unconditional love and service to others. The way to spiritual growth is not through acquisition of material goods and riches. It is not through the desire to have a good time. How often do you hear people discussing the events of the weekend: 'I had a great time. We went to a party and really got stuck into the alcohol. I can't remember half of it, but gee, I know I had a good time.'

Can you imagine any benefit that this attitude has to your spiritual growth? I am not saying we should never go out and enjoy ourselves.

Rather, I'm returning to the constant theme of this book, which is the importance of developing balance in your life.

The way to nurture your spirit is through unconditional love and service to others. Inner peace is not derived purely by spending all your time helping the poor or sick but also through taking time to develop your own personality and character and to look after yourself in order to give yourself the strength to perform unselfish acts.

NURTURING OUR ENERGIES

Each of these five essential energies – physical, mental, emotional, sensual and spiritual – contributes to the overall energy that any one individual has at any time.

How often have you walked into a room and immediately felt uncomfortable – or conversely, and much more positively, walked into a room and immediately felt good, depending on who was in the room at the time? How often have you had a conversation with somebody which left you feeling so drained and tired that you almost needed to go and lie down? Alternatively, how often have you had a conversation with someone which left you feeling alive and stimulated with the desire almost to take on the world? Science cannot measure this transfer of energy from one individual to the next, but there is no doubt that it happens.

I believe that as you have read this chapter, it has become clear to you that it does not taken an enormous change in your life to increase all aspects of your energy levels. Our wellbeing and ultimately our existence is dependent upon the maintenance of our five essential energies. If we are to work towards achieving the Life Factor, it is imperative that we organise our lives so these energies are nurtured and grow.

CHAPTER 3

Fear: Who's afraid?

Fear is the source of our negative behaviours and emotions. Although hate is said to be the opposing force to love, in my opinion it is fear.

We have five basic fears which motivate our negative behavioural patterns:

1 fear of death
2 fear of ageing
3 fear of freedom
4 fear of isolation
5 fear of lack of meaning.

1 FEAR OF DEATH

The prime consideration of every living organism is to survive. One of the main distinctions between human beings and the remainder of the animal kingdom is that we allegedly have the consciousness to be aware of our own mortality.

With the irrefutable knowledge that our physical bodies have a definite use-by date, we progress through our life journey with a background desire (in most cases) to extend this use-by date for as long as is humanly possible, so to speak.

FEARS, PHOBIAS AND NEUROSES

Most of our basic fears, phobias, neuroses and so on are due to this fear of death.

During a recent trip to the Grand Canyon, I realised my lifelong fear of heights was not completely cured. Yes, I still have a problem standing on an unprotected rock ledge peering down a huge chasm. I seemed to be enveloped with a strange sense of foreboding, with thoughts that I might slip, stumble, be pushed or, through some quirk of nature, the rock might split in two at the wrong moment and plunge me to my inevitable death.

As I stood gazing at the splendour of this natural wonder, I realised I derived a strong sense of awe when standing well back on the railing-protected path, rather than anywhere near the non-railed ledge.

Call me a coward, a wimp or any other name you care to mention and I'll accept the label. But, please don't ask me to go abseiling with Tom Cruise (for those of you who have seen *Mission Impossible 2*).

This is not a fabricated fear or some trumped-up attention-seeking device, this is an ingrained instinctual fear of death.

As I have matured, my fear has lessened. Tall buildings, plane flights or peering down stairwells from the thirtieth floor cause me no angst whatsoever. It's not that I'm less scared of death from freefall without a parachute; rather, I suspect that my logical sub-conscious is becoming more discerning in regard to what does or doesn't strike terror in the very depths of my grey matter.

Fear of death can manifest in many bizarre forms. I was once asked my opinion of agoraphobics and my response was, 'Oh well, it keeps them off the streets.' But seriously, this particular phobia, which literally means 'fear of the marketplace', makes the sufferer a prisoner in their own home. The fear of venturing outside the comfort of their normal surroundings is a somewhat convoluted substitute for the fear of death. The perceived danger of losing the security of home, of being 'trapped in a crowd', creates a scenario of danger for the sufferer, tantamount to a mini-death.

Again, the age-old psychological chestnut about nature or nurture – that is, whether you are a product of your genes or your upbringing – commonly emerges when discussing any of mankind's numerous phobias.

Unfortunately in the majority of cases we cannot make an easy distinction. Those people who unwittingly passed on the miscreant DNA that might have led to whatever is the 'phobia of the month' are the same people who nurtured us throughout that often-blamed childhood.

So, who knows – and some would say, who cares? The fact of the matter is that phobias exist and they almost certainly represent our own personal instinctual fear of death.

Interestingly, there is an opposite group of human beings who appear to exhibit no fear of death whatsoever. Some would call them thrill-seekers, daredevils or adventurers, but I call them lunatics. These are the folk who throw themselves out of planes or off cliffs or who climb very tall mountains, experiencing sub-zero temperatures that seriously challenge the blood flow to their limbs. Although these people appear to exhibit no fear of death, they are, in fact, reacting to this basic fear by trying to cheat death with their high-risk behaviours.

So, we're all geared for survival from the day we are conceived and our major fear is about losing the battle to survive.

Our physiology is geared for survival, as I outlined in chapter 1. We have the fear–flight/fight system to allow us to either defend ourselves or run when we're confronted by danger, thus enhancing our chances for survival during these circumstances. And we also have the opposing system that kicks in during relaxation or sleep, shutting our metabolism down to its bare minimum to conserve energy during these down times.

We have a defence system (otherwise known as the immune system) which travels constantly through the body detecting damaged or ageing cells, foreign invaders or substances that are introduced into our body which may lead to harm. When needed, our immune system immediately snaps into action to ensure our survival.

It is clear that all our body's systems are geared for survival, which explains our inherent fear of death. A very common example of this fear in action is the phenomenon of a panic or anxiety attack. This usually occurs in predisposed individuals during times of stress (but certainly can occur spontaneously in some people) and is characterised by a switch on of the fear–flight/fight system. The heart races, there is sweating, dizziness and a dreadful sense of impending doom.

CASE STUDY – BILL

Bill Travers is 62 years old. He is an overweight diabetic who under-went coronary artery bypass grafting over five years ago. Recently he was staying in a small hotel in Paris and in the middle of the night, the fire alarm sounded. Bill jumped to his feet and he attempted to find the fire exit. Eventually, he found the exit but this led to an event he had not experienced previously.

Bill suffered an intense panic attack which, since this initial episode, has recurred when he is confronted with even the most minimal stress.

Why these attacks were triggered from the fire alarm episode and not from any earlier event is a mystery. Panic attacks are, however, often precipitated by a real situation of danger that could possibly lead to death but, once the attacks have begun, they often continue even when there is no reasonable cause.

Fear of flying is a common phobia which can cripple many people's travel plans. Janice used to love flying until one particular trip when the plane hit a rather bad patch of turbulence. Despite this being a normal occurrence on many flights, Janice was convinced the plane was going to crash. From that moment on, any plane flight brought the same response, prompting Janice to avoid flying at all costs.

THE DEATH OF A LOVED ONE

The fear of death comes in many forms but it is still the same basic fear. For however long it has been destined we rent our current body, this fear – overt or covert – will be lurking somewhere, often striking when we least expect it.

If we were to live with the fear of death forever in our conscious mind, existence would be unbearable. We therefore suppress this thought for most of the time until we are confronted by a personal occurrence that brings us face to face with this fear.

When you examine the top ten life crises, the numero uno, Top Of the Pops, is the death of a loved one.

I have experienced such a death now on three occasions. My first experience came one week before my final exams in high school. My best friend, Jack, was tragically killed in a swimming pool accident. As a self-absorbed seventeen-year-old, I was totally overwhelmed. There was no way I was going to be able to sit my exams.

I attended Jack's funeral. I sat through the funeral in a daze. I felt this was a surreal experience. One of Jack's favourite songs that he often played for me on the piano was being played during the service. I stared at the coffin, realising that I would never again see this special young man.

Jack's grandfather was one of the greatest ever Australians. Sir Lorimer Dodds was knighted for his services to medicine. This great man founded the Children's Medical Research Foundation. I had met Sir Lorimer on a few occasions. He was one of those special people who are imbued with enormous dignity, wisdom and peace. He radiated this peace and wisdom with a manner that made you feel very special.

As I left the church, Sir Lorimer was standing at the steps thanking everyone for coming to Jack's funeral.

You would understand and forgive a grandfather for being absorbed in his own grief. I also was in the privileged position of knowing how close Jack and Sir Lorimer were to each other. But when it was my turn to talk to Sir Lorimer, he took my hand and said, 'Ross I need to talk to you.' Immediately I thought, what would this great man have to say to someone like me?

'Ross, you and Jack planned to do Medicine together. Now you have to do it for both of you.'

There I was, caught up in my own grief, being 'hit between the eyes' with one of the most powerful comments (if not the most powerful), that has since influenced my entire life.

To this day, I am practising medicine for two people; Jack and myself. It has been said many times that adversity is a great teacher. It is during times such as these that you are faced with a choice: you can either sink or swim.

Thanks to the inspiration of this great man, Sir Lorimer Dodds, and his grandson, my dear friend Jack, I was able to turn my life around at that moment. I was given a new purpose in life. Anytime my life seems difficult, I remember that purpose.

Regardless of my own personal experience, what does this event say about greatness? Greatness, as exemplified by Sir Lorimer, although certainly measured by his public achievements through his services to medicine, can also be examined at a more personal level.

During a time of enormous personal grief, he was able to step outside his suffering to touch someone else's life and demonstrate an enormous influence for good. Although I considered myself young and unimportant, Sir Lorimer saw me, as he saw everybody, as special. If as we travel through our life's journey we consider each person we meet or interact with along the way as special, we're learning an important lesson – and teaching that lesson to someone else. I learnt that valuable lesson through facing and experiencing the death of a loved one.

My second experience came with the death of my grandfather – my father's dad. I was especially attached to old Pop. Although I have always detested cigarette smoking, some of my fondest memories of childhood came from visiting Pop and Grandma, sitting on the front verandah with Pop whilst he puffed on a roll-your-own cigarette and I slowly sipped Grandma's lemonade.

Pop would espouse his simple philosophies on life and although they were probably not profound, they provided me with a secure bond to this gentle, sweet, old man.

He stopped smoking at the age of 70 when the inevitable emphysema took hold and unfortunately developed lung cancer at 75. His death, in a peaceful coma a few months after diagnosis, seemed a welcome release.

He died as he lived: peacefully and without complaint. I felt sad at his loss, but his age and underlying ailments did not allow me to grieve unnecessarily. I retain only happy memories of a good man who lived life simply.

My third and most painful confrontation with the grim reaper came with the death of my father. Five years earlier, a colonoscopy had revealed the bad news that Dad had colon cancer. A subsequent operation revealed that the cancer had spread through the wall of the bowel.

Dad had recovered reasonably well until he developed a severe depression. Around nine months before his death my mother rang me to tell me that Dad had acute abdominal pain. I suspected the worst and unfortunately my suspicions were confirmed. A CT scan of his abdomen revealed secondary tumours in his liver.

Dad died during my January holidays and I was at his bedside with Mum at the moment of his death.

Although, as a professional speaker, I derive enormous pleasure from speaking to any audience (the bigger the better), when nine months earlier I had realised that Dad had terminal cancer, I lived in dread of delivering a eulogy at his funeral.

However, I felt it was my duty to this man I loved (and still do). So, despite my own emotions, I decided I must speak at his funeral.

Five people would speak for Dad that day: Dad's sister; my sister; my lovely and capable daughter Alexandra, at that stage sixteen years old; my elder brother; and myself. I was to follow Alexandra. She spoke with an elegance and maturity far beyond her years. Her words melted whatever composure I had left whilst I sat in the front row staring at the photo from Dad's earlier, more youthful days that was propped up against his coffin.

My tears began to flow as Alexandra returned to her seat. I walked to the microphone wondering how I could speak, now visibly crying. Dad had told me a few days before his death whilst he was lying on one of those wonderfully comfortable hospital trolleys, 'Ross, I'm a simple man with simple tastes, I want a simple funeral – don't you go spending your money.'

And this was how I started the most difficult speech of my life.

My father was a simple man with simple tastes and simple ideals. As far as society was concerned, Dad was not a huge success. He never earned much money and what he did earn he gave generously to his children, usually to support their education.

Although very smart, Dad came from a poor family and never really had the opportunity he gave to his own children. Dad wasn't famous. He didn't drive a fancy car and did not live in a large, impressive house.

Dad, however, taught me the most valuable life lessons which will hold me in good stead throughout my life. Dad was totally devoted to his family, fiercely loyal and at all times demonstrated unconditional love.

He adored his wife, his children and his grandchildren. Why? Because they were his. Dad didn't have an agenda. He didn't see people for what he could suck out of them.

My dad was basically a good guy. No, more than that, my father was a simple, uncomplicated man – a great person!

Whilst I sit here and write this, the tears are literally streaming down my face. The tears are for many reasons: tears of sadness at my loss, tears of guilt for not living up to these principles at all times and probably tears of remorse because I'd been so busy during my professional working life that I didn't spend as much time with Dad as I wanted and I have not grieved properly for his passing.

My memories of Dad are centred on those simple life principles of loyalty, devotion and unconditional love. I ask you, is there anything more you really need to achieve in your life than being able to display, feel and live these principles?

CONFRONTING THE FEAR OF DEATH

So I have shared with you my personal experiences with the death of three people I love. Yes, I say 'love', not 'loved', because true unconditional love does not stop with that person's passing.

Too often we take for granted those around us with whom we share the most intimate aspects of life. Often, sadly, it is not until they are taken from us by death that we understand the impact our loved ones really do have on our being. The deaths of these three special people have made me acutely aware of the importance of not taking our loved ones for granted.

I still fail, I still make mistakes, but hopefully out there in the ether these three people give me the reality check to guide me back onto the right path.

When I consider my own death, I do not break out the champagne and say, 'Hurry up, I can't wait,' but I also do not live in constant dread. I do, however, realise that all life is lived in the moment. Although we should make plans in all aspects of our life, we also should ensure that we are enjoying and savouring each moment. No-one can travel through life expecting every day to be without problems or challenges. But rather than seeing these problems as obstacles, we should view them as learning experiences and opportunities for growth.

Thomas Edison took around 1500 attempts before he invented the light bulb. When he was asked, 'Weren't you upset that you failed 1500 times?' he said, 'No, I now know 1500 ways how not to make a light bulb.'

I often quote Viktor Frankl and I believe his philosophy is very relevant when confronting our fear of death or the death of someone we love. 'It's not the suffering but the way you handle the suffering that is important.'

Every honest person has a fear of death – either their own or of those they love – but confronting this fear and growing through acknowledging and understanding it is a major step towards achieving the Life Factor.

2 FEAR OF AGEING

Closely aligned to fear of death is the fear of growing old. Often seen by many as a slow death, ageing is not something many of us accept too readily.

I detest those scientists who proudly announce that men reach their peak at 18 and women at 35. What, it's all downhill from there? Thanks very much!

There is no doubt that as we age, most of our systems lose that supple efficiency we possessed in our youth. Our joints ache, we take longer to recover from illnesses and we don't usually sleep as well – still, think what you're doing for the pharmaceutical industry and birthday candle manufacturers!

Society is much to blame for our attitude to ageing. We are bombarded with images of svelte young nymphs on billboards and in lingerie commercials or, for us males, the fit young men with rock-hard abdominal muscles and not an ounce of fat to hang a love handle on.

Over the age of 35, unless we can spend at least an hour a day in the gym, on our bike or pounding the footpath, we start to notice the inevitable weight gain, wrinkles and cellulite.

With the growing emphasis on up-to-the-minute consumer goods comes an accompanying wave of materialism over the importance of a youthful physical appearance. Our use-by dates fast approach, especially when our teenager children constantly remind us of our weight gain, lack of trendiness and basic inability to understand the modern world (as they know it).

Let's face it, growing old sucks if you consider it from a Western perspective. In other cultures, older people are revered for their experience and wisdom. In our culture we see nursing homes as a viable alternative to the extended family.

One of the major consequences of modern medicine will be an increase in the ageing population. I believe the next 50 years will see life expectancy extended well beyond current rates.

At the turn of the last century, the average male could expect to live into their late seventies and females into their early eighties. By the year 2050, with the amazing advances that are on the drawing board at the moment becoming standard therapy, longevity of somewhere between 120 and 150 will probably be commonplace.

Don't, however, assume that this means hordes of decrepit elderly people will be filling the streets, forgetting each other's names and asking directions back to a suburb they haven't lived in for 65 years. I believe that medicine will also unlock the secrets to reverse ageing and all the nasty diseases that go with it. We will then be faced with the problem of overpopulation and lack of resources but I'm hopeful science will invent some creative solution.

But enough of the social comment – that's for the sociologists and philosophers to explore. I'm actually trying to examine the subject at the personal level.

Fear of ageing is like any other fear. We all have them and we must all learn to confront, understand and eventually accept them. Our body ages, but our spirit or soul doesn't. That is why you really don't feel any different now than you did when you were twenty (unless, of course, you are eighteen!).

When we all realise – and I include myself here – that we're not here for material acquisitions and maintenance of our youthful physical appearance but here for spiritual and personal growth, we will be much happier and contented. Life is a journey with a beginning and an end. The end point of life is death, so we should savour every moment of the journey, including the latter part of life.

As we age, our needs change at a superficial level but the two basic needs that never change are our need to love and to be loved. If you are loved purely for your physical appearance and material acquisitions, I would question the depth of those who claim to love you.

Ageing presents many different challenges but these can be summarised into one word: loss. We face loss of our youth, loss of our status, our income, often our close loved ones, and so on. These inevitable losses hang over our head like the sword of Damocles until we reach the point where we accept and deal with them, as we should do for all life challenges.

Is there any major solution to the problem of ageing? Yes, of course there is: it's called acceptance.

CASE STUDY – PETER

Peter Princeton is 56 years old. He is a successful orthopaedic surgeon, well respected by his peers and admired by many grateful patients. He had retained his good looks and despite a busy life had maintained an exercise program that had preserved his slim build.

His wife, however, wasn't as lucky. Although an attractive woman, the combination of a difficult menopause, hormone replacement therapy and an old knee injury led to her experiencing significant weight gain and bouts of depression. With Peter's busy life and 'self' program, he was not a particularly supportive husband. Their sex life was non-existent as Mrs Princeton had lost all interest and Peter was no longer attracted to her anyway, creating increasing problems at all levels of the relationship.

Then along came Janine, an attractive 33-year-old theatre sister who was not backward in her intentions. She had met Mrs Princeton at an office Christmas party and felt this 'pompous, overweight hag' was probably making Dr Princeton's life a misery. Janine decided she would make a not-so-subtle move on the good doctor.

With the deteriorating relationship and lack of sex with his wife, Peter was easy prey and foolishly within a few weeks had fallen for Janine hook, line and sinker.

Peter was fearful of growing old, he did not want his sex life to end and he was unwilling to try to mend a failing relationship with a woman who had supported him through his years as an intern and resident and right through his successful career, not to mention being the mother of his children. Thus began a disastrous period in his life.

He moved out from his matrimonial home to much bitterness and disdain, not only from his wife but also from his children (his eldest daughter being a year older than his new girlfriend).

He moved in with Janine and was totally captivated by her. One year later the divorce was final and he and Janine were married. His children refused to attend the wedding, especially in view of the nervous breakdown suffered by their mother after the end of the marriage.

Peter had basically destroyed his primary relationships, which had been built up through nurturing and hard work based on love, trust and respect. The four people – his ex-wife and three children – who had been the focus of most of his life were lost to him for a number of years, if not forever.

Janine began to feel the maternal urges now she had snared her man. Peter was so smitten he could not refuse her request. So there he was in his late fifties changing nappies and having his precious sleep disturbed, not by a major trauma victim during his on-call service at a large teaching hospital, but by his newly arrived off-spring, 23 years younger than his third child by his previous marriage.

I'm not suggesting it was Peter's fear of ageing that was the major fuel for the fire of this situation but it is certainly a contributing factor. As we age, our needs also change.

Was Peter happier? Initially, most certainly. He was making love to an attractive young woman with a gorgeous body, over twenty years his junior. But, when the novelty had worn off and reality set in, it was clear that he had destroyed his life, big time.

We have all heard of cases identical to Peter's. We all marvel at how seemingly intelligent people can make these decisions.

My response to this story is not one of sanctimoniousness or superiority. I believe every human being is capable of finding themselves in a similar position, given a few impetuous wrong decisions.

This 'Peter Pan' syndrome which unfortunately afflicts so many middle-aged males is based both on a fear of ageing and the 'grass is greener' fallacy.

My mother-in-law, who often comes up with some great sayings, once said, 'Don't try to find your happiness in another person's misery.' I also believe an excellent life principle is that short-term gain usually means long-term pain. In almost all cases, the inability to delay gratification and put in the hard yards causes major long-term problems.

Anything in life that requires hard work and long-term commitment usually offers the greatest rewards. The short-term attraction of material goods, physical beauty (which in all cases doesn't last forever unless you are very good friends with a superhuman cosmetic surgeon) and the other trappings of youth will eventually leave the consumer feeling empty and somewhat short-changed.

One of the most beautiful people I have met is one of my patients whose name is Violet. In her eighties as the name suggests, Violet is a sweet, caring person and has one of the most engaging smiles I have ever seen. Despite a few minor medical problems, she is happy, contented and much more interested in the welfare of others than in any of her own issues.

Of course, Violet is not happy about growing old, but has reached old age with dignity, elegance and an enormous capacity for unconditional love.

I believe the choice is obvious: we can choose love or we can choose fear. Why is it that so many of us choose fear?

3 FEAR OF FREEDOM

Fear of freedom may at first appear to be a rather bizarre concept. Our right to freedom is as ingrained as our need for food and shelter.

But, as the medical intuitive Caroline Myss so rightly states, many people are entrenched in a behaviour she calls 'woundology'. Woundology is a term that describes the way people blame past events for their current traumas and behavioural patterns. The reality is we are free to react to what each day brings, by whatever method or means we desire.

Too often, however, we do not exercise this freedom and appear much more comfortable with the perpetuation of the rules and routines of our past, no matter how damaging or ineffective they may be.

One of my dear friends told me the story of his uncle. He was visiting his uncle's house on a particularly hot day and went to open a window in the lounge room. His uncle proceeded to say, 'We don't open that window, we never open that window.'

'Oh, is it broken?' my friend enquired.

'No, we just never open it,' his uncle replied.

To most of us this window-opening (or not opening) incident seems blatantly ridiculous. But how often do we cling to our own set of rules which, examined objectively, are equally ridiculous?

I was discussing diet with one of my patients and suggested that her husband should not be consuming the enormous quantities of meat that he had eaten for many years.

'Well, what do you expect him to eat if he doesn't eat meat?' she said.

'Why don't you feed him fruits and vegetables with maybe the meat occupying a smaller portion of the plate?' was my reply.

'Oh, he doesn't like fruit and vegetables,' she emphatically stated.

'Really? When was the last time he ate fruit and vegetables?' I asked.

'He never does,' she replied.

'Then how do you know he doesn't like them?' I was fast becoming somewhat exasperated.

'Because he won't like them!' came the bemused answer.

Many people are comfortable with this lack of freedom. We are so often trapped by our routines and life habits. We often lack the desire to be free. In fact, as I mentioned in chapter 1, many people suffer anxiety from the excessive choices now so common in all aspects of society.

There are now so many varieties of every consumer product that often this freedom of choice creates excessive anxiety and therefore fear.

But we can't go back to the good old days when life was easier and simpler. I agree there were some advantages to that lifestyle but we also must be realistic. The reality is that we are living in the twenty-first century with all its options. This fear of freedom means we never really take the time to learn what options are available to us. Our fear prevents us from breaking through to a different way of thinking.

It's so easy for us to blame our parents, past events or other external situations for our own particular behavioural aberrations. It is much harder to admit that we have the freedom to say, this is my problem, regardless of the background factors that may have led me to this point. It is our responsibility to deal with our problems, using whatever skills and means are available to us.

4 FEAR OF ISOLATION

One of the greatest pleasures for most people is sharing our lives, our experiences and happiness with others.

From the moment of conception, we are joined to another person. When we are born we immediately begin the bonding process with our mothers and to a lesser, though still important extent, our fathers.

We spend our entire lives developing relationships: with family, friends, work colleagues and those with whom we choose to create long-term and lifelong partnerships.

Human relationships are an integral and motivating force for most people.

Therefore, a major fear for many of us is the fear of isolation, of being alone. Often many people choose a destructive relationship rather than a life of peaceful isolation.

CASE STUDY – JULIE AND STEPHEN

Julie is 45 years old. Following a long but unrewarding relationship with her first husband, Julie left the marriage when her children had reached adulthood.

After a few years of living alone, Julie met Stephen. Stephen was a very overpowering person and decided that they should tie the knot.

Stephen was a dentist. Although very competent, he always had a penchant for women and throughout his career there had been some question as to his relationships with some of his female patients, especially those requiring sedation for the more invasive dental procedures.

He was, in fact, charged and suspended for sexually interfering with a patient who was under sedation. This incident and numerous other allegations created an enormous strain on Stephen and Julie's marriage.

Stephen, who would be described as character-disordered, denied any wrongdoing. Julie's reaction to the situation (so said Stephen) was clearly neurotic. Julie was not showing Stephen the loyalty he deserved, so he thought.

After months of court appearances that made them minor celebrities with the press, the strain was clearly showing on both Julie and Stephen.

When Stephen's appeal against his suspension was turned down, Julie had had enough and moved out.

Initially Julie was happier. She no longer had to endure the constant badgering and abuse by Stephen. She no longer felt the invasion

of her personal (both physical and emotional) space that was a
feature of the relationship with Stephen.

But Julie was alone and without funds. Although Stephen was
suspended, he had established considerable wealth from investments.
When Julie moved out, her finances contracted. The lack of money
and the loneliness, not to mention Stephen's persistent phone calls,
lowered Julie's resistance and she moved back with Stephen.

As far as Julie was concerned, the loneliness was intolerable.
Many people would argue that living alone would be better than
living with Stephen. However, such pronouncements glibly under-
estimate the profound effects that loneliness can have on different
individuals.

Variation of personality type is one of the aspects that make life
so fascinating. Our immediate and long-term needs, our desire for
companionship, will vary according to our basic personality type
and life experiences. Some people are very content with their own
company and would, in fact, prefer to be alone. I would venture to
say these people are the exception rather than the rule. Basically
most of us need to feel loved, wanted, needed by others.

This extends to our feelings of self-worth, even if the situation
does not seem particularly emotionally healthy. Having someone
depend on us is usually better than being alone. People have no
right to judge another person's choices under these circumstances.

Fear of loneliness is a powerful motivating factor for many
people. The need for contact with others is firmly rooted in human
behaviour, not only at a communal, tribal level but also, of course,
at a more intimate, personal level. There is almost certainly an
instinctual need for contact and nurturing as seen in all animal
species. This need becomes a prime reason for existence.

Many older people say they don't feel needed any more. One of the
enormous benefits of the extended family is that grandparents retain
a vital connection to the family, especially to their grandchildren.

A common scenario is what I call the 'retirement syndrome'. Once a couple has reached retirement age there is often a desire to move to a quieter life in the country.

CASE STUDY – ERIC AND ROSEMARY

Eric and Rosemary decided in their mid-sixties that they had had enough of city life. Eric had finished his career as the assistant manager of a large retail firm and hated the constant traffic problems, the pollution and the ever-increasing threat of violence, theft and so on.

Living in the city was becoming increasingly expensive and although his superannuation package was quite healthy, he was concerned about making ends meet.

Rosemary, however, was more reticent about moving. They lived relatively close to their three grandchildren and Rosemary regularly minded the youngest child for her daughter.

Eric was insistent they would have a better life if they retired to a coastal town 500 kilometres from the city. He would enjoy maintaining a larger property now he was retired and they could spend more time travelling with more available funds not being eaten up by city expenses.

Rosemary reluctantly agreed, much to her daughter's dismay. They sold their house, made a healthy profit and moved to the coast.

Within weeks of moving into their five-acre property, Rosemary felt isolated. Eric had joined the local golf club and when he was not on the course, he was spending most of his time in his yard, maintaining the property.

Rosemary, on the other hand, had made no friends and most importantly no longer had constant contact with her daughter and grandchildren. Eric remained insensitive to Rosemary's predicament, claiming, 'This is the best move we have ever made.'

The more Eric seemed to be settling in, the more unsettled Rosemary became. The isolation and loneliness were becoming overwhelming. Any suggestion by Rosemary about a return to the city was laughed off by Eric.

'You'll get used to it,' he would say whenever the topic was raised. 'I'm not sure I want to,' would be Rosemary's reply.

Within six months, Rosemary's health began to suffer. She began to wake at 2 or 3 am, finding it hard to return to sleep. She developed a persistent rash which did not respond to a variety of creams and ointments prescribed by the local doctor.

Rosemary began experiencing panic attacks at the local super-market or in restaurants. Antidepressants were prescribed which lessened her symptoms but did not treat the true underlying problem. Her fear of isolation was now a reality that could only be resolved by a return to the life she enjoyed, where she felt useful and wanted. She needed contact with the people who needed her.

Eric acted as if Rosemary was a live-in housekeeper. He derived all the companionship he needed from his mates at the golf club. When he was not on the course or in the garden he would prefer to watch the television rather than sit and talk with Rosemary. For the most part, conversation between Eric and Rosemary consisted of his complaints about the constant long-distance phone calls to their daughter, which were costing a fortune.

At the bottom line Eric and Rosemary's move was a win–lose situation. In the city, Eric was unhappy but in the country Rosemary was not only unhappy, she was also desperately lonely and as a consequence, was becoming ill.

This retirement syndrome is very common. My advice to people considering a major life change is to think very carefully before making a commitment. The idyllic retirement plan may be fraught with danger. To leave a situation where you have strong social supports purely for the prospect of less traffic and pollution or a few dollars saved may see you looking down the barrel of loneliness, isolation, increasing medical bills but often lesser availability of medical services. I'm not suggesting that a big move following retirement is always a bad decision but many people do not consider the potentially negative outcomes.

Perhaps the most profound and realistic fear of isolation comes with those who are dying. Regardless of the strength of our social supports, we must all face death alone. There is no real solution to this fear because, like fear of death itself, there is no denying the fact of mortality.

The need for human contact and the need to feel useful, to feel needed, is basic to most human beings. The very real fear of isolation deserves recognition by us all. This fear becomes reality, especially in groups such as the elderly. It behoves all of us to realise that even a simple smile or polite conversation with a stranger may be enough to, at least temporarily, allay this fear.

Let's face it, we're all in this life together; all part of the huge functioning organism called Earth. In reality, no one person really needs to feel isolated. It is such a tragedy of the human condition that so many people suffer this fear.

5 FEAR OF LACK OF MEANING

For those of you who have read *The Hitchhiker's Guide to the Galaxy* by Douglas Adams, you will recall the answer to the meaning of life is 42.

The big issue, however, is, what is the question? Does life have a meaning? Is there a grand plan? Is there a God who directs our lives, creates situations, dramas and traumas to make a long and sometimes arduous journey less than routine? Although many people are convinced – due to their upbringing, personal experiences or even a sense of inner knowledge – that this is the case, in reality no-one can be 100 per cent sure of God's existence.

Even those who claim to have witnessed supernatural phenomena such as ghosts or ESP, clairvoyants who have accurately predicted future happenings or those who have suffered the vivid reality of near-death experiences are now being discredited. The scientific world claims there are designated parts of the brain which, when stimulated, can create any of the above experiences. The effects of hypoxia (lack of oxygen), temporal lobe epilepsy or schizophrenia can easily explain any phenomenon the paranormalists care to espouse.

This reductionist view of the world, where everything has (or will at some stage in the future have) a scientific explanation, is simplistic to say the least.

Unfortunately, however, our rationalist scientific era has created scepticism in many circles. It is now a widely held notion that if something can't be proved by science, it either will be in the future or it just doesn't exist. If you can't see it, hear it, touch it, smell, or taste it, or even better, test it in a laboratory, then it doesn't exist. If we live our life by the scientific model, where we are the biological product of the union of our parents' DNA and we will, after an unspecified number of years, die through accident, misadventure or disease, we would have to accept that the sole purpose of our existence is a recycling of carbon and other molecules and maybe a bit of fun along the way.

It is precisely this hypothesis, put forward by many in the world of science, that accentuates the final of our five basic fears.

What if there is no meaning to life? What if we are basically slugging it out on the planet with the only decent oxygen supply in the solar system just to contribute our little bit to the hole in the ozone layer? Nature can also be cruel in its randomness, adding fuel to this argument. A parent burying a young child can be forgiven for doubting the presence of meaning to life.

A meaning to life or true life purpose does not mean a spiritual presence or influence in all cases. The dependence or love of those around us may be enough reason for us to see meaning in our lives. A worthwhile occupation or a life passion can instil a sense of meaning, even without belief in a higher power.

Regardless of the persuasive arguments of various religions, theorists and sceptics, all questions pertaining to the meaning of life will remain unanswered until the moment of our death. Then we'll either know or we won't.

If the self-assured, rational humanists are right, at the moment of death they won't even be able to gloat because – guess what – they'll experience nothing, just as they predicted.

But just imagine how stupid they'll feel if they're wrong – they'll really feel like a right bunch of Charlies.

On the other hand, for those with a deep personal belief that there is a God and a life beyond this one, at the moment of death this knowledge will be forthcoming. If, however, they're wrong – well, what does it matter? They won't find out that they're wrong. They'll come to the end of the road and move into that rather long stretch called Nothingness, so they won't have to put up with any heckling from the 'I told you so' humanists!

But it is that lingering doubt, that inability to be 100 per cent sure, that fuels this particular fear. We all know that death is a certainty (how many times have you heard the old death and taxes line?) but fear of lack of meaning is almost the opposite.

Without wishing to advocate self-deception, my suggestion to combat this fear is to simply develop some meaning in your life.

I'm not suggesting that if you are a committed atheist, a 180-degree turnaround to become a religious zealot is the way to go. Your atheism itself may give your life some meaning. It is the passion you have for your opinions that is most important.

An atheistic mother may find all the meaning she needs in her love for her children. So the point I'm trying to make is, regardless of what happens at your life's end point, it is really your decision right now as to whether your life does or doesn't have meaning. Just make the decision to be certain about something and follow through with your commitment.

One of the major problems with most of us (and I'm not suggesting yours truly is any different) is that we do our best (often without trying) to complicate our lives through taking on too many commitments, projects, relationships and so on. The simpler we can make our own life with simple beliefs, aims and opinions, the less stress, fear and complications will occur.

CREATE MEANING IN YOUR LIFE

So make the decision right now to believe in something, as this belief gives your life meaning. Keep this belief simple and avoid placing your faith in material goods. It is belief – in principles, in love, in a higher being, that takes away our fears.

When there is meaning to your life, you have a yardstick, a barometer, a secure place in which to nurture your behaviour and feelings. So, whatever meaning you decide upon, don't see that as a means to an end. It is an end in itself.

CHAPTER 4

Early days: Laying the foundations

When I asked one of my friends, who is a well-respected paediatrician, 'What is the essence of good parenting?' his reply was very straightforward. Good parenting is based on two simple concepts: love and constancy. If a child feels loved and receives consistent discipline and messages from his parents, the chances are that he or she will turn out okay. What do you want from your children anyhow? Not every child can be a Mozart or an elite athlete; nor should we expect them to be. I believe all we can expect from our children is that they can find happiness and satisfaction in their lives.

THE INFLUENCE OF PARENTING

I must say from the start, however, that I do believe it is the way we are parented that determines our behavioural patterns for the rest of our days – unless we make a conscious decision to change our behaviour in some way. This is not just a personal belief of mine. It has been confirmed by many psychologists and theorists.

CASE STUDY – LEON

Leon is the eldest of four children. He is nineteen years old with a sister who is fourteen and two brothers aged ten and eight. For the first five years of Leon's life, his young, enthusiastic parents went overboard in the attention department. Leon's mother used flash cards, ensuring he could read by age three. His home library was choking with books and his father ensured he could kick a ball and hold a bat as soon as he took his first steps. Leon basically suffered from attention overload but as a child of five, he felt this excessive attention was completely normal. Since birth, he had been totally primed to be the centre of attention without having to compete with anyone.

Then disaster struck! Along came little sister. We all know what happens when a baby arrives. They demand attention – and lots of it.

I'm sure you can guess what happened next. Leon became very unhappy. All of a sudden, he had to share his mum and dad with a little screaming, eating, crapping and sleeping machine. Leon was no longer the centre of attention and he found this very unfair. He also had to cope with his first year at school where he was in a class of 30 and the teacher didn't realise that he was a superstar who deserved special attention and consideration.

But the scene had been set. Leon performed well academically throughout his school years and was talented at sport. Outside the home, he had a close circle of friends but still those old childhood interactions would plague him. Problems he encountered would create tension and subconsciously maintain the anger he had felt ever since the birth of his sister. Leon was great when alone with his parents, but at times was an intolerable brother, forever teasing and intimidating his younger siblings.

When Leon experienced any stress, such as just before exams or more mundane examples such as an argument with one of his many girlfriends, he had such a short fuse he would rapidly lose his temper and revert to the bratty, angry five-year-old.

On the positive side, Leon was a successful student with ambition. But he is also a very good example of how the way we are parented can have profound long-term effects – bad and good.

Although Leon's parents had the best intentions, they were young and green at the job and went overboard with the attention. It gets back to the age-old theme of balance. Even too much of the right stuff can cause problems. Although feeling too loved and too special would be the envy of many children, it can still cause problems for those who are brought up in this fashion. They can find it difficult to assume their natural place in the world, or to be part of a team. Their own ego and its stimulation is the main focus, overshadowing other issues.

If you see your life as you would the building of a house, the first five years are like the foundations of that house. Once the foundations are in place, it is very difficult to change the structure of the house. Ninety-five per cent of the influence in our first five years of life comes from our major role models. This influence continues up until the teens and by then it is very difficult to change. So if you intend giving your children constancy and love, it has to start from day one. Children's brains are like sponges; they absorb almost everything put before them.

I have rarely seen a drug addict or an alcoholic who felt genuinely loved by his or her parents. I have rarely seen a patient with intense neurotic problems where I could say there was a family atmosphere of constant loving and consistent discipline. Of course, individuals can project inaccurate perceptions of their family situation; nonetheless if the perception exists in the mind of that individual, it has a tangible impact in their life.

What about the family that appears to have only one defective member, the so-called 'black sheep'? Surely this aberration has to be due to some problem in the genes or just plain bad luck. Again, this may be an explanation, but not one particularly shared by the psychiatric and psychological community. Virginia Satir, in her book *Family Therapy*, suggests very strongly that a defective family is the problem, not a defective gene or person. She states that the family will treat the troubled member as if they are a patient. They will use them almost like a garbage dump, offloading on them all their own neuroses. If people can say, 'It's not my problem, it's their problem,' then they feel much better.

CASE STUDY – SELF-CONCEPT

I once had a patient who in her late thirties was unmarried and came to see me because of a lifelong history of palpitations (an abnormal sensation of the heart beating). She stated that she came from a Mediterranean family with a very volatile, aggressive father. Every time there was a family conflict, she would feel her heart race and would become very weak and look very grey. Her mother told her she had a weak constitution and would never be strong enough to raise a family. She carried this belief into her thirties. She went to a general practitioner complaining of palpitations and was referred to me. When I listened to her story, I realised immediately she was suffering from a condition known as supra-ventricular tachycardia, which is an abnormal racing of the heart caused by an extra electrical circuit.

I then informed her she was born with this condition and that she was not neurotic, as she believed, but it was just that any anxiety would provoke this electrical circuit to work, causing her heart to race. She then realised that her problem was a physical one.

With this realisation that she was not neurotic, and using her own personal resources, she was then able to change her belief system and self-concept. I organised effective therapy for her heart condition and her symptoms settled. She has since married and had a child, and is extremely happy.

This woman should not have had to go through years of suffering at the hands of a misinformed parent. What we say to our children can have a profound effect on the way they see themselves for many years to come.

One of the major skills of parenting is to realise that each child is born with an individual character. These individual characters each need to be nurtured. Allowing children to grow up in a positive environment is vitally important. If a child continually sees their major role models – usually their parents – being negative, then what else would you expect from the child? If that child is always positively encouraged and made to feel special, then this can only have the desired effects.

Let's face it, as adults we love encouragement, so imagine how much children love encouragement. How many times every day does a small child say, 'Watch me, Dad, watch me, Mum'? They want and need reinforcement on a constant basis. If they get negative reinforcement, then the negative behaviour will be reinforced. These explanations are so simple, but so true. I believe the reason why many of us find them so difficult to accept is because we do not want to take responsibility for some of the less acceptable behavioural patterns we see in our children.

In certain dysfunctional families, as stated earlier, there is only one person who is seen as the patient and this person takes on all the problems for that family. Other families, however, are so defective that either every member of the family has some enormous problem or, even more interestingly, there is one member who stands out from all the rest.

CASE STUDY – THE SHEEHAN FAMILY

Phil and Jean Sheehan were young when they married, 20 and 19 respectively, and in fact they did not marry through choice but because Jean was pregnant at the time. Both Jean and Phil were devout

Catholics and abortion was out of the question. They had a beautiful baby daughter and over the next ten years three more children followed. Although Phil was a devoted husband, Jean was extremely difficult to live with. She was very moody and prone to inappropriate outbursts of anger, then at other times was inappropriately affectionate.

Through her childhood and teenage years, Carol, the Sheehans' eldest child, became the 'rock of the family'. She excelled at school, coming first in most subjects, and at home was expected to perform a significant amount of the housework, along with minding the younger children. Basically Carol was not allowed to have a proper childhood.

Despite this, Carol continued to support her very difficult mother, her only refuge being the last few years of high school when she developed a very strong social network. At least she could escape her mother's constant demands and at times bizarre behaviour. This behaviour was not only directed at Carol, but also at the younger children. Jean was extremely jealous of her children's relationship with their father and would often make inappropriate comments, at times of a sexual nature, regarding Phil's relationship with his younger daughter.

Phil spent many hours away at the hotel with his friends, leaving Jean alone. In turn, Jean then expected Carol to help her cope.

Despite her difficult childhood, Carol graduated from high school and then gained honours in law at university. She met and married another law student and had three children. She is now in her thirties and intends to recommence a law practice when her children are well entrenched at school.

Carol herself has many subtle neurotic problems such as a fear of death, manifested by many psychosomatic symptoms. She makes constant visits to the doctor, only to be reassured on each occasion there is no sign of physical disease. Despite these problems, on the outside she is an extremely successful and wonderful mother to her three children.

Her two brothers and her sister, on the other hand, have battled drug addiction and alcoholism and one has attempted suicide.

The argument of Carol's brothers and sister would no doubt be that people are born the way they are. There is no doubt that each of us is born with a certain character and some characters are much stronger than others. The way we are parented, however, can make or break these characters and it is the skill of parenting to know your children's strengths and weaknesses and to emphasise their strengths and to support and downplay their weaknesses.

One of the first twin studies looked at a pair of identical twins who had been separated at birth. One twin had been placed in an allegedly supportive, caring family and the other in a broken home. The study found, in this particular case, that the girls had grown up with very similar psychoneurotic problems. Unfortunately these studies will always be flawed as, first, it is impossible to extrapolate from one case to many others, and second, a seemingly supportive family may still have many hidden problems. It could be that the adopted twin entered the good family and became the 'patient' for the rest of the family, such as I have already mentioned.

It has been said of parenting that we are all victims of victims and the only way to break this ongoing cycle is to change the way we react to our children. We should not see the guidelines given to us by our parents as the only guidelines that we can use for our children.

Our development as a person depends very much on the following factors:

1 female role models
2 male role models
3 position in the family
4 sex of the child
5 life experiences – good and bad.

1 FEMALE ROLE MODELS

Your lifelong relationship with your mother is pivotal to all other relationships. The bond between a mother and child will often determine the character of other relationships. A mother, in the emotional sense of the word, is the provider of security, comfort and unconditional love. Mothers able to demonstrate and offer these three important aspects of a child's existence will provide a solid foundation for the rest of that child's life.

Unfortunately, over the last 20 to 30 years there has been an erosion of the importance of motherhood which, interestingly, has coincided with rising societal problems. As women are made to feel less than important if they are not in the work force, and as the need to support a family financially (especially in single parent families) increases for many reasons, the energy needed to nurture children with the above characteristics is diminished.

I believe this is one of the contributing factors in drug abuse, youth suicide and the pervading sense of hopelessness increasingly seen amongst teenagers and young adults. Their mothers are expected to be Superwomen. They must run a household, nurture children, have a paid – often full-time – job, not to mention be ideal passionate lovers to their husbands.

Not too many people can fulfil all these roles, nor should they be expected to.

2 MALE ROLE MODELS

With the increasing rate of separation and divorce, many children are growing up without regular input from a male role model. I believe an important contribution to a child from the male role model is confidence.

The father or male role model can either make or break a child in this regard. It you feel valued by your father as a child, you will usually consider yourself a valuable adult.

3 POSITION IN THE FAMILY

You may find this an odd inclusion, but I believe this is also a very important contributing factor to personal development. Your position in the family often determines your responsibilities as a child and the nature of your relationships with your parents and other siblings. We too often hear of the 'responsible' older children, 'the middle child' syndrome and the 'baby' of the family.

It is important to remember that as you negotiated your childhood, your parents were often traversing their own issues through different stages of their lives. Their levels of maturity, work and life experiences often may have influenced their attitudes and efforts as parents at that particular time.

The young, ambitious father may often transform into an older, more hands-on parent and thus (just to give one example), the parenting styles within the same family could change completely over time.

4 SEX OF THE CHILD

Regardless of how much you care to deny it, we all tend to treat boys and girls differently. Hormones and traditional role models very much impact on expectations and parental behaviour. There are also a number of well-conducted trials demonstrating distinct sex-related behavioural patterns commencing at a very early age. One simple study showed that male infants will venture further from their mothers than female infants. Aggressive behaviour is more common in male toddlers.

5 LIFE EXPERIENCES – GOOD AND BAD

Sometimes in life we get lucky breaks and at other times it seems we draw the short straw. As I repeat constantly throughout this book, it is the manner in which you react to these life experiences, good or bad, that will determine the nature of your journey.

Your life experiences as a child are seminal in shaping your future. That one failure at school where you were made to feel less than adequate may lead to avoidance of any similar activities as an adult.

Alternatively, praise for one type of activity may accentuate your enjoyment of this activity and lead to your seeking experiences and possibly employment related to this activity. At an acute level, the premature death of a parent often changes the behaviour of a child, permanently.

With increasing urban sprawl, children often grow up having less contact with grandparents. Many years ago, the nuclear family often saw grandparents living in the same house or usually very close to the children and grandchildren. These days it is often the case that grandparents live at a great distance from their grandchildren, perhaps even in another city. The retirement dream of moving out of 'the rat race' to a quieter existence often means that grandparents see their grandchildren less frequently. With the burgeoning divorce and separation rates, often contact with the 'in-laws' is lost. The typical tension between an estranged or divorced couple may lead to the severing of ties between children and one set of grandparents.

This is, of course, not always the case and there thankfully will always be situations where grandparents play a central role in the development of their grandchildren.

Relationships between siblings are also vitally important in determining the emotional growth of the family and the individuals within it. Teenage tensions between siblings will often melt to be replaced by strong bonds as adults. In many cases, the old adage of 'blood is thicker than water' prevails.

I travel throughout the world lecturing on stress management. During my lectures I say to the audience, 'Raise your hands the people in this audience who come from dysfunctional families.'

When a few honest people raise their hands, I make the following statement, 'The answer is that 60 per cent of people come from dysfunctional families and 40 per cent are liars.'

In reality we are all 'victims of victims'. No-one can truly say that they had a perfect upbringing because, for all the reasons we've already explored, no-one is perfect.

Despite carrying the title of cardiologist, I'm still a doctor and have long had a keen interest in the psychospiritual basis of disease. I have seen numerous dysfunctional families where it was clear that one member, the 'patient', had been singled out to become the emotional dumping-ground of other family members. Interestingly, the other members of the family were very quick to tell me they had no problems. Instead 'he' or 'she' – the patient – had always suffered from this or that condition and was a constant burden to the family.

CASE STUDY – DANIEL

Daniel is 23 years old. His father, Brian, had been a strict (some would say tyrannical) man who expected nothing but optimum achievement from his children. Daniel's older brother, at the age of 29, was completing his training in surgery, whilst his older sister was happily married with two children at age 30.

Despite being very bright, Daniel had hated and shied away from any kind of academia. He had barely passed his final exams at high school and drifted from one job to another, preferring to smoke marijuana and watch television as his two main forms of recreation. He was a constant disappointment to his father and in many ways Daniel had spent his life ensuring this would be the case.

Following a heavy weekend on the 'evil weed', Daniel started hearing voices and hallucinating. A diagnosis of acute schizophrenia was made and Daniel was admitted to a psychiatric ward in a teaching hospital.

At the time I met Daniel, I was a medical student working in psychiatry and I well remember his case. I also distinctly remember his family. His mother and father went to great lengths to try to convince the psychiatry team that Daniel was a disappointment in an otherwise very successful and well-adjusted family. The concern appeared to be focused on proving the worth of themselves and their other two children rather than the speedy recovery of their wayward son.

At that time, I had been studying Satir's work and it occurred to me how relevant this case was in demonstrating a dysfunctional family with a clear-cut 'patient'.

In many ways, your relationships within the family can be your foundation for success or the shaky start to a very rough and at times painful, difficult road. Carl and Brendan, whom I refer to in the introductory chapter, had the same father, but Carl used his dysfunctional upbringing as fuel to strive for a better life. Brendan, on the other hand, constantly used his negative childhood experiences as the excuse for his behaviour.

This is the pivotal importance of decision and awareness – they allow you to see your early life as important 'training' on your path to achieving the Life Factor.

CHAPTER 5

Am I stressed?

Is stress just another yuppie phase or is it a true disorder that can cripple people's lives? There are many unanswered questions about stress and it is my aim in this book to offer you a practical and easy-to-read approach to understanding stress and coping with this ever-increasing problem.

Let's begin by looking at some case studies that clearly demonstrate the serious havoc that stress can wreak in our lives.

CASE 1 – DON

Don is a 42-year-old medical specialist. He is at the peak of his career and is certainly one of the top specialists in his field. He is a lovely, personable fellow who is well respected by his peers and loved by his patients. He exercises regularly, is an excellent tennis player, consumes a good diet and enjoys a very contented family life.

Don, however, arrives home at between eight and nine o'clock every night during the week and is often called out after hours and on the weekend. For two years, Don has had recurrent chest and abdominal pain. His symptoms have been fully investigated with exercise testing and heart scans. He has even had tubes shoved into his major orifices to check for possible problems in his gastrointestinal tract. Despite these extensive investigations, no abnormalities were found in Don's case.

Although enjoying the wealth, popularity and professional success that most people could only dream about, why is Don still plagued by pain?

Stress is like a stone in your shoe. It doesn't matter how much you build up the shoe, if you don't remove the stone it will still irritate you in some fashion. Don's major problem is that he works far too hard and has lost the balance so necessary to achieve peace and inner contentment. For Don to overcome these symptoms, he needs to make some serious life decisions about the amount of work he takes on. This is a very common problem amongst professional people.

CASE 2 – KAREN

Karen is a 46-year-old woman who was diagnosed with diabetes at the age of 42. At that stage she was a thin, attractive woman who looked ten years younger than her age. Soon after the diagnosis of diabetes, she had recurrent bouts of chest pain and was found to have minor blockages in one of her arteries. Over the next couple of years, she gained 10 kilograms in weight, partly because of the effects of insulin but due in large part to the fact that she did not change her dietary habits and started to drink excessive amounts of alcohol.

Karen is an intelligent woman who takes pride in her appearance but she found it far too hard to cope with diabetes and the drastic changes it brought into her life. Her behaviour means she is on a self-destructive path that will surely end in a major complication such as a heart attack, stroke or even possibly the loss of one of her legs from the complications of diabetes. Why can't she change?

Up until the diagnosis of diabetes, Karen's life had travelled rather smoothly. When confronted with such a dilemma she found it very difficult to cope with this enormous imposition on her life. For her to change will require significant decisions and awareness of the consequences of her current behaviour.

CASE 3 – PHIL

Phil is a 39-year-old executive in an insurance firm. He has worked his way up from a junior position to one of authority through hard work and dedication. Phil, however, is very unpopular with his staff.

Although he is very efficient and, one would say, obsessive at work, he is also a very angry and hostile person with a very short fuse. He drives his staff to be as time-urgent as he is, so it is no wonder there is a high turnover of work but also of staff in his department.

Even more disastrously, he has carried on his anger and hostility at home. He is now separated from his wife and two children. He had been married at the age of 26 and his relationship broke down ten years later. Although he was never violent physically, he was constantly unsupportive and very demanding of his family. Despite this, he had absolutely no insight into his behaviour and still to this day has no idea why his wife left him. Why has he no insight and why can't he see that it is his problem and not the problem of those around him?

Phil is a classic character-disordered male. His inherent personality type along with defective childhood priming have created his current adult dilemmas. Without developing a serious awareness of his own faults, he will continue to blame all of his life's dilemmas on other people.

CASE 4 – ANGELA

Angela is a 54-year-old patient of mine who was initially referred with unusual chest pains, palpitations (rapid racing of the heart), and recurrent bouts of shortness of breath and dizziness. Despite thorough investigations and recurrent admissions of Angela to hospital with these symptoms, no cause was ever found.

Angela sits in my waiting room at times, waiting for her next appointment, working herself up into a frenzy worrying about what nasty condition I might find she has today. At every consultation, she has a list of around ten to twenty questions and always I find nothing wrong with her. I reassure her, she temporarily feels better and leaves.

Although Angela has a very supportive husband, I discovered over numerous consultations that she had a very troubled childhood. I confronted her with the fact that there is nothing much wrong with her and told her in my opinion her problems were related to stress. She was quite bemused by this and said she was one of the most relaxed people she knows. Why can't she recognise how anxious she is and do something about it?

Angela is a classic neurotic. Her childhood priming has obviously set her up for this behaviour. Constant reinforcing of the 'medical model', where she describes her symptoms to health professionals who then carry out investigations to find a physical cause, strengthens Angela's belief she has a significant medical complaint. Helping her understand her childhood reactions to her adult problems and minimising her medical investigations are important strategies in her case. Unfortunately, although her husband is supportive, her symptoms are also a form of attention-seeking to which he readily responds.

CASE 5 – MARCUS

Finally, and probably the most perplexing case of all, is that of Marcus. Marcus is a 59-year-old man who has had more stress in his life than most people would have in twenty lifetimes. He was a refugee from Poland and came to Australia a number of years ago, settling in a coastal town in New South Wales. Marcus's son developed a brain tumour at the age of five. He had neurosurgery, radiotherapy and chemotherapy and his brain tumour went into remission. During the three years that Marcus and his wife battled to support his son, his wife contracted breast cancer and after a very painful year or two, died. Soon after his wife's death, his son succumbed to the brain tumour.

Throughout all these traumas, which would have plunged most people into depression, alcoholism or drug addiction, Marcus found meaning in his suffering and despite his obvious sadness grew through all of his bad experiences.

Since the death of two of the three most special people in his life, Marcus has spent most of his time trying to help other people who have had to endure the same kind of suffering. He has been and will continue to be an inspiration to many people. What is it about Marcus that makes him different to the other people who suffer similar types of stress but give in to the pain?

Marcus is a classic example of a special person who can work through stress and emerge stronger and more effective. Although suffering numerous tragedies, his life paradoxically has been enriched by his ability to react in such a fashion to these stresses.

BECOMING AWARE OF STRESS

'I can handle stress much better than the next guy,' you might hear people say. Another beauty is, 'I don't suffer stress at all.'

This blissful ignorance of one's own condition allows many people to suffer a myriad of symptoms from which the medical profession enjoys a steady income stream. Millions of dollars are spent investigating headaches, chest pain, gastrointestinal disorders and other symptoms troubling individual patients. Many of these symptoms are stress-related.

Every single person who lives in this society suffers some degree of pressure. That pressure may come from your family. The pressure may come from work. The pressure often comes from your-self. Regardless of its source, the pressure is still there and has to be recognised. This pressure becomes manifest in many different forms: physical symptoms, psychological symptoms or whatever your poison is in terms of drugs of addiction – all are equally disabling.

PHYSICAL PRESENTATIONS OF STRESS

A man went off to the doctor and said, 'Doctor, one night I dream I am a wigwam and the next night I dream I'm a tepee.'

The doctor said, 'I know your problem, you're too tense.' [2 tents]

A joke, of course – but stress can present in a myriad of ways. Indeed, one person's stress can be another person's joy.

Stress can also manifest itself in bizarre ways. The most unusual presentation of stress I have ever seen occurred in a 34-year-old lady referred to me for assessment. Her major symptom was long-standing pain down her right arm. She had seen numerous other specialists and was diagnosed with many different types of spasms. Muscular spasm, oesophageal spasm, coronary spasm, here a spasm, there a spasm, everywhere a spasm, spasm!

In my discussions with this lady, I realised that her symptoms were not at all physical. I felt that she had some stress-related disorder. I asked her about her life and she said, 'Don't start this stress business with me, doctor, there is absolutely nothing wrong in that department.'

When I witness such adamant denial regarding stress, I am immediately alerted to the likelihood that the patient has a signifi-cant stress-related disorder. She went on to tell me how she was happily married with two small children and life was wonderful. I said, 'Okay, things are great at home but what about your friends?'

She said, 'I don't have any friends.'

'Well, you don't have any friends now but did you ever have any friends?' I asked.

She said, 'Yes, but I don't want to talk about it.'

I knew I was close to the problem so I focused on the friends she once had. Eventually she admitted to me that when she was seventeen, she was standing at the bus-stop with her best friend who had just been given a new bracelet. My patient wanted to try on the bracelet and grabbed at this girl's arm.

Unfortunately the girl pulled back, slipped and fell under a bus and was killed. I then asked my patient, 'What arm did you grab your friend's hand with?'

She looked down at her right arm with the immediate realisation that happens in these situations and began to cry uncontrollably.

In psychiatry, there is a term known as abreaction, which is the bringing to the surface of suppressed painful emotions. The outpouring of emotion meant that the emotional pain this girl had been hiding for so many years was now brought to the surface and relieved. After that profound reaction, my patient had no further chest or arm pain and continues to do well.

So what physical symptoms can be attributed to stress? Basically any symptom from your head to your toe can be caused by some form of stress. The reason for its localisation to a particular area may be due to childhood conditioning, a genetic weakness or prior injury to one particular area, causing this area to be predisposed to suffer in times of stress.

Common presentations of stress may include recurrent headaches, facial pain, chronic sinus problems, a chronic or recurrent sore throat.

Hoarseness of the voice is another common stress-related phenomenon, as can be fluctuations in the intensity of the voice.

Chest pains, palpitations (experience of the increased sensation of the heart beating), shortness of breath (often manifesting as hyperventilation), or recurrent episodes of dizziness can also be stress-related phenomena.

A very common manifestation of stress is recurrent gastrointestinal problems. This can be anything from oesophageal pain to recurrent abdominal pain, chronic diarrhoea or constipation.

One of the most common diagnoses in medicine is irritable bowel syndrome. This is not a truly pathological entity. When the bowel is biopsied or examined under a microscope, it is entirely normal. Despite this, the person definitely experiences recurrent bouts of abdominal pain and intermittent changes in bowel habit. This is often a stress-related phenomenon and treatment of the stress can often relieve the gastrointestinal symptoms. Recently, however, some researchers in Australia have discovered a parasite known as *D. fragilis* which has been implicated as a significant cause for irritable bowel syndrome. Further research needs to be performed in this area.

Chronic muscular pain, or pins and needles in the hands and feet can also be manifestations of stress.

STRESS OR SERIOUS DISEASE?

Despite the many symptoms that can be attributed to stress, it is vitally important that a doctor does not blame every single symptom on stress. It is not infrequent that people are told they are suffering a stress-related disorder when they are actually suffering serious disease.

CASE STUDY – LARRY

Larry Greaves is 53. He was under incredible stress at work and started to develop chest pain. The pain was not related to exertion but would often occur during particularly stressful days at work. It would manifest at times as a tightness and at other times as a gripping feeling over his left wrist. He visited his doctor who reassured him that it was purely related to stress.

Larry initially accepted this diagnosis. For the following few months, however, Larry's pains increased in severity and one evening following a particularly busy and upsetting day at work, Larry was sitting at home watching television and suddenly developed a severe pain in the centre of his chest.

He called his wife, who saw that he was sweating and looked grey. She promptly called the ambulance. When the ambulance arrived,

Larry suffered a cardiac arrest and fortunately was resuscitated. He was admitted to hospital and treated for an acute heart attack from which he recovered completely.

Unfortunately, some people are not as lucky as Larry. They can be told that their symptoms are stress-related, and then when they suffer an acute event, they do not even make it to the hospital. Unfortunately one in three people die from a heart attack before they arrive at the hospital and this problem needs to be addressed.

Usually a careful history taken by a competent doctor can determine stress-related problems, but if there is any suspicion whatsoever, such as a new pain occurring in a person over the age of 35, this needs further investigation.

The techniques for assessing heart disease are improving all the time. Now, with high-speed CT scanning of the coronary arteries and the newer technique of arterial tonometry, heart disease can be detected years and at times decades before it manifests.

Regardless, if you're suffering any new symptoms from your head to your toe that cannot be easily explained, I would suggest an immediate assessment by a competent doctor. Of course, if you suffer a bit of burning in the centre of the chest every time you have a hot Indian curry, this is almost always due to indigestion and does not need further investigation unless it is increasing in severity.

GASTROINTESTINAL PROBLEMS

One of the most common reasons for a visit to a doctor is some sort of gastrointestinal problem. This can be anything from a lack of appetite, indigestion or abdominal pain to intermittent diarrhoea or constipation. It is interesting to note that even within the same person, these symptoms can vary.

Investigations by the medical profession include referral to a specialist gastroenterologist or colorectal surgeon. Patients undergo many investigative procedures in the search for some reason for the chronic debilitating symptoms. For many of these patients, however, abnormalities are never found and they are plagued by recurrent problems. Various diagnoses are made from nervous dyspepsia to irritable bowel syndrome to spastic bowel and oesophageal spasm. I believe almost every human being has experienced one or another gastrointestinal symptom at some time in their life. Too many of these people tolerate the symptoms without even bothering to seek a doctor's assessment.

HOW MUCH INVESTIGATION IS TOO MUCH?

There are two main issues that need to be addressed when medical investigations are carried out. The first issue is, how do we know when our condition is purely stress and not something serious? The second issue is, how do doctors know how far to investigate people? We all remember the epitaph on the hypochondriac's grave that says, 'See, I told you there was something wrong!'

The medical profession does not want to be accused of being too casual in their approach to people with recurrent symptoms. However, there is also no justification to investigate every single person who believes there is a problem just because the person is certain the doctor is missing something.

WHEN ARE ONGOING INVESTIGATIONS CALLED FOR?

So how do we know what is stress and what is a serious underlying disease that may be being missed? How far should doctors investigate the symptoms of the hypochondriac who is convinced they have something wrong, even though the doctor is certain their symptoms are purely psychological?

Firstly, there are many disease patterns that can be determined by doctors through a careful history, examination and appropriate tests. If these tests have been performed to the best of the doctor's ability and no abnormalities have been found, it is highly likely that the person does not have a physical problem that needs treatment.

To give you an example, say if someone presents to the doctor with chronic abdominal pain centred around their navel. The pain has been present for over twelve months, is not associated with weight loss and does not have a particular relationship to precipitants such as food, exertion, body position or bowel action. In such a case, it is unlikely – although not definite – that the condition has a sinister cause.

If the person has had tests such as an endoscopy (the insertion of a slender instrument, known as an endoscope, through the mouth into the oesophagus and stomach for the purposes of examination), an ultrasound of the gall bladder and possibly a CT scan of the abdomen, along with appropriate blood tests and all of these are normal, then they can be reassured.

I am certainly not suggesting that all of these tests are necessary in every person with symptoms. The most important aspect of assessment includes a very careful history and physical examination. In over 90 per cent of cases this can point towards a firm diagnosis. The tests are purely there to confirm the diagnosis and to give the doctor and patient an indication of the severity of the condition, if it exists at all.

MEDICAL SOLUTIONS ARE ONLY PART OF THE STORY

Why does it appear that the medical profession is not particularly good at dealing with problems related to stress? I think stress is difficult to treat because many of the precipitating factors for the stress response are events over which doctors have no control.

For example, a middle-aged woman attends the doctor with a story of chronic abdominal pain for which thorough investigations have all turned up normal results. She then offers the information to the doctor that her husband has a drinking problem and one of her teenage children is on drugs. A low dose of anxiety-relieving drugs such as a benzodiazepine is purely a Band-aid to a much deeper and more far-reaching problem. One of the great dangers in labelling someone with a stress-related disorder is that the physical cause is ignored.

An analogy to stress is that of a bridge with a structural fault. If one person at a time walks across the bridge, no great strain is placed upon the bridge and it functions quite well. If a large crowd of people crosses the bridge, it puts an enormous pressure upon the bridge and it will crack where the structural weakness is present. This is exactly what happens in the body. If we have a structural weakness anywhere, then the stress will precipitate a manifestation of this weakness.

Whether a symptom is purely a stress phenomenon or whether there is an underlying physical component, that symptom can nevertheless be quite disabling. So, either way, it is important for a doctor to make a thorough evaluation of any symptom a person has and to manage that symptom appropriately. In Part II, I discuss ways to deal with stressful situations and offer some plans for those affected.

PSYCHOLOGICAL PRESENTATIONS OF STRESS

Stress-related symptoms may also manifest as psychological symptoms. A person might say, 'I am so worried about situation Y or person X.' The reality is that they are worried and are trying to hook that worry onto something or someone. We have such a variability of human experience and human response that what may worry one person may have absolutely no effect on another person. The worriers, of course, feel that those who don't worry are uncaring and insensitive to difficult situations. The reality is that the worrier has been taught from an early age that the way to deal with difficult situations is to worry about them. But we all know that we benefit zero from worrying about any situation. Of course, when a problem arises we need to consider it carefully and deal with it, but worry and concern do not help resolve the matter.

PANIC ATTACKS, PHOBIAS AND ANXIETY

Recurrent panic attacks, phobias or chronic anxiety can all be manifestations of underlying stress. It is usually external pressure that precipitates these symptoms but the problem is often much deeper and usually stems back to childhood behavioural patterns.

DEPRESSION

Another complicated illness, and one which is often bound up with stress, is depression. There are two main types of depression. The first is known as reactive depression and the second is endogenous or chemical depression.

REACTIVE DEPRESSION

Reactive depression occurs as a grief response. When any bad situation happens in our life we feel sad about it, and in turn this can cause depression. The death of a loved one is a very common and obvious example. When you lose someone, you feel acute grief.

Elizabeth Kubler-Ross discussed the grief response as occurring in five stages, which can be present in varying order. They are anger, denial, bargaining, depression and finally acceptance. A grief reaction to an upsetting situation is common and normal. There is no drug in the world that can make you feel better about something bad happening; all it can do is slightly lessen your anxiety. It is normal to feel grief when someone dies or someone betrays you. That grief often manifests initially as anger.

When a loved one dies, often the first response of a close relative is anger towards the medical and nursing staff that they did not offer the appropriate amount of care. They are often looking for someone to blame.

I have a lovely aunt who is one of the most caring people you could meet. Her mother died at the age of 85 from an acute cardiac illness. My aunt has punished herself for many years over her mother's death, convinced that she could have done more to save her mother's life. This anger at herself was completely unfounded but was part of the obvious grief response that she suffered.

When someone betrays you, for example if your partner commits an act of infidelity, your anger is obvious and justified. The human brain, however, is a fascinating piece of equipment. The anger in these types of situations will often evolve to the subsequent stages of grief.

The best treatment for acute reactive depression is time, but counselling and cognitive behavioural therapy (CBT) are also useful adjuncts in helping a person cope with the very real effects of grief.

As time goes on, each person must learn to forgive, even if it means forgiving someone who has died. I know this sounds quite bizarre, but when you lose someone to whom you are very close, you do need to forgive them and you need to forgive the people involved in their death. If you carry anger and guilt with you, all it does is punish you.

ENDOGENOUS DEPRESSION

At the other end of the depression spectrum is endogenous or chemical depression. There are so many misconceptions regarding this form of depression in our society. How often do we hear of the person who comes home with a shotgun, shoots the family and then turns the gun on themselves? This not uncommon and very concerning scenario is almost always caused by an endogenous or chemical depression.

As we have discussed in earlier chapters, the brain works by sending chemical messages throughout its very complex system, using a series of chemicals known as neurotransmitters. Our mood is controlled by these chemicals and in particular by a substance known as serotonin. Another group of chemicals also contribute; they are called the catecholamines, better known individually as adrenaline and noradrenaline. If the level of these chemicals in the brain drops, then the affected person will develop endogenous depression.

This is a disease similar to any other disease affecting the body, only in this case it affects the brain. Depression has long had a social stigma attached to it because people perceive depression as a form of weakness and not really a disease state. You rarely hear someone say, 'Oh, that person is weak because they've developed diabetes.' But endogenous depression is exactly the same type of disorder, only it affects the brain and not the pancreas.

There are only three ways to treat endogenous depression. The first and most unsatisfactory is time, because as time goes on, the depression may lift. The second way is with a group of very effective drugs known as antidepressants. Recently, several drugs which directly affect serotonin have been released onto the market and these drugs have minimal side effects and are very effective in restoring a depressed person back to a normal state. They are very commonly used; some would say overused. Nevertheless, they have been very effective in preventing people progressing to severe depression, the major complication of which is suicide.

The third, more intrusive and controversial, method for treating endogenous depression is electroconvulsive therapy. This involves a general anaesthetic and the application of electrodes to the skull. An electric shock is delivered to the skull and this induces an epileptic seizure. This method has been shown in cases of severe depression to cause some improvement. There are, however, reported episodes of significant memory loss after such therapy.

Although counselling and CBT allow a person with endogenous depression to gain more insight into their condition, these modalities have little impact on raising the levels of serotonin in the brain, and therefore will probably not be major factors in a person's recovery.

The common factor that precipitates endogenous depression is acute trauma, either psychological or physical. The death of a loved one may precipitate endogenous depression. Of course, when a loved one dies it is normal to feel depressed but if there are symptoms and signs that this has become a very severe depression, then a diagnosis of endogenous or chemical depression must be entertained and the sufferer treated appropriately. Common symptoms and signs of depression are early morning wakening, a feeling of fatigue, loss of appetite, and a loss of interest in all aspects of life which continues above and beyond what one would normally expect for the normal grieving process.

Many common physical illnesses and major surgical procedures have also been implicated as triggers for endogenous depression. A study from the *New England Journal of Medicine* a few years ago reported a 40 per cent incidence of varying degrees of endogenous depression after coronary artery bypass grafting. These features were present as long as five years after the surgery. Pneumonia or severe viral illnesses can also lead to the onset of endogenous depression. Endogenous depression may be the presenting symptom for different types of cancers, even prior to the diagnosis.

GET A MEDICAL OPINION – AND START MAKING CHANGES

Clearly, stress and symptoms of physical and psychological disease processes manifest themselves in similar ways – often there is a direct link between them. The fact that there are so many possible causes for any symptom highlights the importance of obtaining a thorough medical assessment by a competent doctor when any new symptoms arise in your life.

In my long career, I have witnessed many disasters relating to non-medical people making their own diagnoses, either through disordered intuition, misinterpreting self-help books, comparing their symptoms with those of friends or relatives, or, perhaps worst of all, taking advice from the non-medical next-door neighbour who has set themselves up as an expert on any matter to which you would care to listen. So, please, if in any doubt whatsoever, see your doctor!

Now we will explore ways of coping with stress and even bene-fiting from it by achieving life goals and learning valuable life lessons. You'll find that you will experience tremendous personal growth in every aspect of your life. You'll begin to really feel the benefits of the Life Factor in action.

PART II

The
LIFE
FACTOR
SOLUTION

CHAPTER 6

Goal-setting

When Martin Luther King stated in his famous speech, 'I have a dream', it became one of the most quoted phrases of the twentieth century. We all have dreams, both when we sleep and also during our waking hours.

We dream about working less, owning a big house, a better car – and the list goes on. Unfortunately for most, these dreams never materialise into reality. To make your dreams reality, you need to turn your dreams into goals.

ACHIEVING THE LIFE FACTOR THROUGH GOAL-SETTING

Goal-setting is the first step in my five-point solution to creating a stress-free life and achieving the Life Factor. There is strong evidence that goal-setting produces results. In a study undertaken to examine goal-setting among Harvard University graduates, a group of graduates was surveyed to determine the number who actually set specific, written goals. Only 3 per cent of the group had specific, written goals for the future. After ten years, this 3 per cent had earned more money than the remaining 97 per cent who had not set specific goals.

Now, I'm in no way suggesting financial gain is or should be our only measure of success but it certainly is one measurable parameter and something to which most of us aspire.

FIVE KEY AREAS FOR GOAL-SETTING

For goal-setting to be effective it must cover all aspects of our life. We should be setting goals in the following areas:

1 physical
2 mental
3 emotional
4 financial
5 spiritual.

1 SETTING PHYSICAL GOALS

I once saw a patient who was one of the wealthiest men in Australia. He had more money than most people could even dream about. He had, however, suffered multiple heart attacks and his heart was working at around 10 per cent of its normal capacity. This man could not walk down to his letterbox to collect his mail. He was basically bed-bound because of his severe heart failure.

Without physical health, without sound specific physical goals, there is no real point in making goals in any other areas of your life. If your physical balance is lost, you cannot hope to achieve any of your goals in the other aspects of your life. You should set goals in the following physical areas:

▸ ideal weight
▸ fitness
▸ muscle tone
▸ energy levels
▸ disease prevention.

THE FIVE STEPS TO USE WHEN GOAL-SETTING

In all aspects of goal-setting, we need to adopt the following five steps.

I will use the setting of goals in our physical areas to demonstrate these steps.

Goal-setting should be considered in the following order:

1 decision
2 write it down
3 what is necessary?
4 plan
5 action.

1 DECISION

The first step in goal-setting is decision. You must decide exactly what it is you're trying to achieve. Therefore your goals must be:

▶ clear
▶ specific
▶ measurable
▶ time-bounded
▶ achievable.

Take, for example, weight loss. To say you want to lose weight is a vague, non-specific dream. If, however, you state that you want to lose 10 kilograms over the next twelve months, this fits the criteria seen above. This is certainly a decision that is clear, specific, measurable, time-bounded and, with the correct weight loss program (note that I did not say 'diet'), is achievable. You can use these criteria for any aspects of your goal-setting exercise.

Obviously goals such as fitness, muscle toning or energy cannot be measured as accurately as your weight. Nevertheless, certain aspects are measurable.

If you decide to start an exercise program (and it is my firm belief that all of us should), it is important to follow these guidelines: if you have any symptoms (for example, chest pain, shortness of breath, palpitations or dizziness) or you are over 35 and haven't had an exercise routine for years, consult your doctor and have a preventative assessment. (The details of such an assessment are fully presented in my previous book, *The Cell Factor*.) Once you have started exercising, you should learn how to take your pulse. Most people know someone with a medical or quasi-medical background who can teach you how it's done – it's very simple to learn. (If, however, you are anally-retentive, you might decide to purchase a heart-rate monitor, which will automatically measure your pulse while you're exercising.)

Measuring your recovery time after exercise, before and after a fitness program, is a very useful guide to your level of fitness. This is as simple as checking your pulse three minutes after exercise cessation. If it has dropped back to within 20 of your resting pulse, you have achieved excellent fitness levels. If, however, your pulse is still greater than 100, three minutes after exercise, you should either look at a preventative assessment or at least ease slowly into a fitness program.

Muscle tone can be gauged for men simply by assessing the size of your 'love handles', the tone of your abdominal muscles and biceps. Exercise physiologists and personal trainers can give even more specific assessments by measuring percentage body fat and muscle tone.

For women, in addition to the above parameters, the presence or absence of cellulite is a good indication of muscle tone.

Energy levels are more difficult to objectively quantify. Simple questions can be of some assistance. How do you feel when you wake up in the morning? How long does it take you to feel you can face the day – if at all? Do you get sleepy after lunch? How quickly (if at all) do you fall asleep in front of the television? Do you feel energetic, with a zest for life?

If most of your answers to these questions are negative, you need to bring in some strategies to firstly find out why your energy levels are low and secondly to improve them.

Finally, goals in disease prevention are also achievable. You may have a strong family history of heart disease or an exaggerated fear of cancer. This constant concern may be alleviated by using modern techniques to measure your true risk for these diseases and then commencing specific, measurable steps to achieve this disease prevention.

The steps are specifically discussed in my previous book, *The Cell Factor*. The information in that book and the following information in this book will put you on track to your goal of achieving balance in all aspects of your health, including prevention of common diseases.

2 WRITE IT DOWN

The second step in goal-setting is to write it down. Committing your goals to paper is a powerful step. I believe it is important to keep a record or a journal of your goals. I will go into more detail about this written record – which I call the Life Journal – a little later on. Making small cards that you can keep in your wallet or purse and refer to throughout the day reinforces your goals in both your conscious and subconscious mind. This constant reinforcement makes your goals tangible, real and certainly achievable.

It is also important to reinforce these goals with affirmations and visualisations. The subconscious mind cannot tell the difference between fact and fantasy. If you state your goals in the present tense, as if they are already happening, or visualise the achievement of your goals, this will increase the likelihood of these goals being realised. Once your subconscious is primed into believing goals are being achieved, they start being achieved. The subconscious goes to work to ensure every opportunity is explored. There is more on visualisation later in this chapter.

3 WHAT IS NECESSARY?

The third step to use when goal-setting is to decide exactly what is necessary to achieve your goals. What changes and sacrifices must you make to ensure success? What will you have to give up? For example, to develop a new skill takes time and effort.

Some of your relaxation time will have to be abandoned so you can take the time to learn this new skill. You'll need to spend more time reading about all aspects of this new skill, attend courses and seminars, spend time on the internet and speak to experts in the field. This extra time is to be found in your current busy schedule.

Make an extensive list of the new, necessary steps that will help you achieve these goals.

4 PLAN

The fourth step when goal-setting is your specific plan. You would not build a new house without a plan and equally you cannot achieve a new goal without a plan. Plans should be systematically formulated using the following steps:

(a) priorities for goals
(b) sequence of steps to achieve goals
(c) possible roadblocks and risks
(d) why are you not there now?
(e) action.

Priorities for goals

If you have as one of your goals the desire to be healthier, you must ask what are your major priorities for achieving good health? Say, for example, you are overweight and a cigarette smoker. One of the major concerns of smokers who are trying to kick the habit is weight gain after smoking cessation. This is a real problem and it occurs for three reasons:

▸ Food tastes better when you stop smoking and therefore you eat more.

▸ After stopping smoking you feel the need for oral gratification; that is, something in your mouth. You often replace the cigarettes with food.

▸ If you have ever killed a fly with fly spray, you'll know that they do not go quietly – they buzz and fly around the room at a furious rate. This is because the poison in the fly spray uncouples the metabolism of the fly, sending it into overdrive. In a similar way, smoking creates a state of chronic poisoning, where your metabolism is constantly overworking. When you stop smoking, your metabolism temporarily slows down, and with slower metabolism it is easier to gain weight.

If you are already overweight and you smoke, you must decide which of these two adverse health behaviours you wish to tackle first. Both can cause long-term serious health consequences; I believe the decision is up to you. But, remember, to maintain your current weight after you stop smoking will require a degree of calorie restriction and an increase in exercise.

Sequence of steps to achieve goals

Following closely after identifying your priorities is the sequence of goal achievement. Break your specific goals into steps and list the sequence of the steps you must take to achieve each goal. If your goal is to improve your fitness level to the point where you can compete in a race or recommence playing competition sport, list your strategies to achieve this fitness in order of importance and with a specific time sequence.

Committing the steps to paper strengthens their importance in your mind and increases the likelihood of your success in achieving these goals.

Possible roadblocks and risks

In my opinion, one of the greatest minds of the modern era is Dr Edward de Bono. He introduced the concept of lateral thinking and has elevated to new heights the teaching of 'how to think'. De Bono's techniques allow us to view, in a very ordered and logical fashion, the process of thinking. One of his superb concepts is that of the 'six thinking hats' to use in problem-solving. I have modified this concept to (of course) a five-step approach to solving problems – in case you haven't noticed, my preference is always for five.

I have coined this the FLECA approach:

    (i) **f**acts
    (ii) **l**ogical positives and negatives
    (iii) **e**motive issues
    (iv) **c**reative ideas
    (v) **a**ction.

I have introduced this useful approach to considering any issue in your life at this juncture because I believe it is important to consider all aspects of a problem. If you analyse the possible roadblocks and risks of any new versus old behaviour, you are equipped to deal with these issues if and when they arise.

For example, your new goal may be to stop smoking. You are determined and have developed a new focus in regard to your health. Your first decision and priority is to stop smoking, but what may go wrong?

Write down the roadblocks and the risks of stopping. For example when your goal is to stop smoking, the major roadblock might be that many of your friends are smokers. You know they will feel uncomfortable around you if you are not joining them as you have always done. One of the major characteristics of humanity is the pack mentality. (Pardon the pun.)

Many people like and feel comfortable being part of a group. If you support the same team as someone else, you feel bonded with that person. Alternatively, if someone is from a different culture, country or even community, we humans tend to have an inherent suspicion towards that person. In the same way, the Friday evening ritual of a few drinks and cigarettes engenders a strong bond between any group, which is broken immediately one of the group tries for whatever reason to change the ritual.

Your desire to break the cigarette habit may be viewed subconsciously by your friends as an attempt by you to break the bond of friendship. This is an excellent example of a roadblock to achieving your goal. How you deal with this situation is an important step towards the achievement of your goal. Only you can identify the specific roadblocks you may need to confront.

De Bono would consider these roadblocks as the logical negatives of a problem and probably the emotive issues you need to consider and deal with.

So what about risks? There are many risks to your new behaviour which may impede your success. One of your goals may be to abandon a career you have followed for twenty years and take up a new challenge. This challenge, although exciting and interesting, may mean a significant drop in income. It may involve a new business that is untested in the market place. Who may oppose the business? What is the competition? Basically, I'm asking: what can go wrong? Something that seems so good, seems so beneficial, no matter what, always has a negative side and this must be considered.

Why are you not there now?

What is it about your current life situation that has prevented you from achieving this goal already? Maybe you were happy with your life until recently and a possible change of direction has only become apparent because of a new occurrence in your life.

The much-discussed concept of the mid-life crisis resonates in this situation. There is no doubt that we progress through stages on this fascinating path we call life and it is important we do not let ourselves become stuck in a rut at any point along this path.

Analyse your current situation. Frankly consider what has stopped you up to now in the achievement of these goals and work towards change.

5 ACTION

Whether considering the five steps to use when goal-setting, the FLECA approach to problem-solving, or your specific plan for a particular goal, the last step is always *action*. You can consider your goals, your plans and your roadblocks as much as you like but without action, nothing will change. Follow the steps set out in the five-step action plan which follows shortly, and I guarantee you'll start to notice enormous differences in your life.

Let's now deal with the specifics of goal-setting in the other four areas.

2 SETTING MENTAL GOALS

When we lead a fulfilled life, we learn from life's challenges and we see every day as an opportunity for improvement. Unfortunately, so many people see life as a struggle and most days as just another period of drudgery they have to endure. There is also a common misconception (part of this same negativity) that as we age, our intellect declines. If you accept this, it will certainly happen. If, however, you continue to stimulate the brain every day, in as many ways as possible, you will improve your intellect as you age. One of the most important roadblocks to setting new goals in this area is habit. The older you are, the more set you are in your ways and routines. Thus, the less flexible you are, the less likely you are to try new things and therefore, the less likely you are to challenge and stimulate your mind.

If you see every day as an opportunity for learning you will definitely experience a remarkable difference very quickly.

Although I encourage relaxation I do not encourage wasting your time on activities that are of no value. The modern obsession with television is a great example of a true time-wasting activity. It has been estimated that the average person living in Western society can watch anywhere between 4 to 30 hours' television per week.

Even if you are on the lower end of this statistic, were you to spend these four hours in an active learning activity, can you imagine the improvement in your mind power?

Develop some goals in this area. Start to read challenging books, take seminars in subjects that interest you. Use your time alone in your car to listen to an audio tape or CD involving a learning topic. Talk to experts in the area of your interest and ask as many questions as possible.

Learn a new language. If you learn five new words per day, that is over a 1000 words in twelve months – that's enough to make you fluent in any language.

Start setting yourself goals in all aspects of mental development and I promise you a new intellectual sharpness will quickly become apparent.

3 SETTING EMOTIONAL GOALS

It may seem a bit contrived and impersonal to set goals for our emotional life but without these steps we may well take our emotional side for granted. Often the people we love the most are the ones that are neglected in our quest for a better job, more money or even that extra time to pursue a hobby or a sport.

I personally find it hard to comprehend the person (usually a man) who works ten to twelve hours per day when they have a partner and young children at home, and who will then spend a few hours a weekend playing golf or engaging in some other activity that leads to even more time away from home.

Putting pen to paper regarding your true emotional goals may put this type of behaviour into perspective.

It will not be the board of directors standing around your hospital bed when you have your heart attack. It is unlikely to be your golfing buddies crying the loudest at your funeral. The people you love are the ones who deserve the majority of your time and energy.

Write down exactly what you would like in regard to your

emotional life. How can you improve your important relationships? Are you spending enough time with the people who really count in your life?

4 SETTING FINANCIAL GOALS

The last thing you need is for a doctor to offer you financial advice. I would certainly not even try, but one thing I will say most definitely is that you should set clear, specific, measurable, time-bounded and achievable financial goals. Set out a six-month, twelve-month, five-year and ten-year plan, satisfying all the above criteria.

One of the finest books on money that I have read is *The Richest Man in Babylon*. This book offers many sound financial principles which will hold you in good stead for the rest of your life.

5 SETTING SPIRITUAL GOALS

Without a higher purpose, life has little meaning. Again, it is not my place to push any specific religious barrow but I'm happy to state my position. I'm convinced, as much as one can be in such an imperfect world, that there is a higher being which is the driving force of life in the physical world.

I believe a communion with this higher being gives life meaning and that living by spiritual principles allows us to strive to be better people. Setting goals with these principles firmly in the foreground will contribute to a better life for all. Another important principle stemming from living for a higher purpose is that of service. If we see serving others as being part of living for a higher purpose, life becomes less stressful. Set goals to become more of a giver than a taker. Set goals to spend more time in quiet communion with God.

How do you go about
putting your goal-setting
into action?

1 **PREPARE**
2 **PREVENT**
3 **PROTECT**
4 **PRACTISE**
5 **PACE**

1 PREPARE

It is vital to prepare for your new goals. Use five starter questions: what, how, when, who and why (and sometimes where) to formulate answers to what you're truly trying to achieve.

- Have your specific goals set out on small cards you may even like to keep in your wallet or purse.
- Identify what has worked for other people. Look at mentoring, books, audio tapes and CDs, and courses.
- Revisit your goals and plans on a daily basis.
- Logically sequence the events and steps.
- Examine the consequences of your new goals.

2 PREVENT

When you examine the consequences of your new goals, it is also important to predict the roadblocks or the negative consequences that may impede your path to success or arise as a consequence of your achieving success.

If you wish to start a new career for any reason, you may not be receiving appropriate support from your partner. For example, your partner might counter your suggestion with an argument such as,

'It's a risk, you are making good money and we need to pay the bills. Sure, it might work out, but it might not, and at least now we know how much we are getting.'

On the other hand, your new job may be making you more money than your old job but you are now spending so much time away from the family, it is placing a great strain on your relationships. All these possibilities need to be considered as a consequence of your making changes to your life.

Write down a list of all the possible positive and negative consequences of whatever goal you are striving for. Write this list in each of the five categories of your life.

What are the positive and negative consequences to your:

▸ physical side
▸ mental side
▸ emotional side
▸ financial side
▸ spiritual side?

The last one is particularly interesting to consider. For example, say you have trained yourself for a managerial position in a large financial firm. This position offers you an enormous amount of extra income but more time away from the family, impacting on your emotional side. More distressing, however, is the fact that the firm has a reputation for being ruthless with its employees. The managers are expected to carry out, at times, behaviours towards the employees which are callous and uncaring. These expected behaviours may certainly conflict with your higher values and need to be deeply considered before you embark on this career move.

3 PROTECT

As your goals are new, you need to protect them using the following strategies.

▶ You will often forget your new goals. Prepare 'memory aids' to remind you of your new path. Many people stick Post-it notes on the bathroom mirror, in the car, in their purses or wallets, on their desks at work or in the home office, to act as a constant reminder of their goals.

▶ Declare your new goals to your friends and family so they can assist and support you in achieving success.

▶ Control the environment so everything is manageable. It might not be a good idea to begin a new job when you have just ended a longstanding relationship, for example. Fresh starts are important, but not all at once.

▶ Reward yourself – both physically and psychologically – for achieving new goals. Deprivation is not a reward and this is why most diet programs don't work. Rewards are part of our normal physiology and therefore are very important. Deprivation is not part of our physiology.

▶ Be realistic. Too many people expect too much, too soon. You will often be unsuccessful initially but if you keep trying you will turn things around. The body needs to be trained. Even the 'number one' in the world at any sport has to spend many hours training for the performances witnessed by the public. For your personal achievements to be successful, you require the same dedication to training.

4 PRACTISE

Talking about training brings us to the next point. Practice does make perfect. Seek any opportunity to practise aspects of your new goals. If you know you have to give a speech, stand in front of the mirror and give the speech to yourself first. Do you have any irritating mannerisms that are likely to drive your audience crazy? Are you using phrases like 'you know' or saying 'err' too often? Do you appear animated or is your voice dull and monotonous?

Practise the lecture on your friends. Discuss all aspects of your new goals at any opportunity.

5 PACE YOURSELF

Set a realistic time frame to achieve your new goals: the slower, the better. Constantly observe your progress and record this progress in your Life Journal (see below). Ask for feedback about your progress from others. Ask your mentor, your coach, your personal trainer, your loved ones: do they think you are working towards achieving your new goals?

YOUR LIFE JOURNAL

I suggest that you set aside some time now to create a Life Journal. Choose a journal format that suits you and is accessible, so that using the journal is always a positive experience for you.

A loose-leaf folder allows you to add or subtract when new goals supersede the old. For the technophiles amongst you, a computer is an excellent tool to use in creating and keeping a Life Journal.

Once you have established your Life Journal, create separate sections for your physical, mental, emotional, financial and spiritual goals.

I know what you're thinking – this creates yet another duty in an already stressed and busy life. In reality the journal should only take about half an hour to one hour to establish and then consist of only five to ten minutes' review time every day; maybe even less.

For such a powerful, life-changing technique, can you afford not to spend that time?

When considering the Five-Step Action Plan it is also important to adopt five key action steps:

(a) DAILY REVIEW OF ALL GOALS

Your major life goals need to be reinforced. The simple act of disciplining yourself to review these goals on a daily basis imprints them in your mind, almost like a mantra.

(b) DAILY REVIEW OF YOUR PLAN

Your goals are powerful single-sentence statements of what you're trying to achieve in all aspects of your life. Your plan is the means to achieving these goals. Summarise your plan in your Life Journal and spend a few minutes every day in reviewing this plan. One of the greater success techniques in any field is reinforcement and follow-up. In the marketing world, if you don't remind your clients of your service at least once every three months, you are soon forgotten.

(c) TAKE SMALL, MANAGEABLE STEPS

Confucius once said, 'A journey of a thousand miles begins with a single step.'

Commit yourself to some action towards achieving your goals on a daily basis. If your goal is to write that one great story or novel, one page a day every day for twelve months will mean you have achieved a 365-page novel in one year. Not bad for around fifteen or twenty minutes' work per day.

Cutting back a twenty cigarettes per day habit by one cigarette a day will mean you have stopped smoking within twenty days. Such is the power of small steps.

(d) VISUALISE GOAL ACHIEVEMENT

Many high-level athletes will visualise their gold medal winning performances on numerous occasions prior to the competition. Visualisation trains the subconscious mind and therefore the body for success. Whatever your goal, spend a few minutes sitting quietly with your eyes closed, imagining you have already achieved this goal.

VISUALISATION

Visualisation is a powerful healing technique which I personally have witnessed completely reverse an otherwise hopeless situation such as terminal cancer.

The important principles of visualisation are as follows:

▶ You must create, with your eyes closed, a vivid picture in your mind of the outcome you desire.

▶ You must add the emotional soundtrack. Not only is a vivid mental picture vital, the vivid emotions associated with this new behaviour or situation are also very important. You must absorb yourself in the situation, making this new behaviour real.

▶ Create this new behaviour in the present tense. Believe it is happening now and not at some designated time in the future. Your subconscious mind cannot tell the difference.

▶ Practise. Discipline yourself to spend 5–10 minutes every day in visualisation. When you practise this technique you will find that you will achieve your goals.

The only limit to your success in visualising anything is the limit you place on your own imagination. Life is, in many ways, an illusion where we are limited (if we allow ourselves to be) by our receiving system, better known as the sensory system. Our five senses – sight, touch, hearing, smell and taste – are the way we interact with our environment. We have absolute freedom, however, to react to this information and process these factors in whatever way works best for us.

Obviously, the stronger the sensory information, the more difficult it is for us to react in a neutral fashion. A pungent odour, treading on a thorn, a deafening noise, or a very bright light usually provoke reactions in most people.

Most of the time, however, we are not exposed to such strong stimuli. Therefore, without these strong stimuli interfering with our normal neural (nervous) processes, our brains are free to react in individual fashion.

Enter our imaginations. We can basically imagine ourselves in any situation with no limits. You can imagine yourself as a person you truly admire: perhaps a famous statesmen or sage. How would Gandhi react in this situation? Would Winston Churchill have felt negative about this dilemma?

So, when visualising, realise you have no limits to your imagination.

(e) MONITOR YOUR PROGRESS

There are two aspects of monitoring your progress – self-monitoring and feedback from a more objective source. Let's face it, it's your goal and therefore your opinion is the most important. Record your progress in your Life Journal and make this as quantitative as possible. If weight loss is your goal, record this on a weekly basis in a prominent place so it is very easy for you to monitor your progress.

If you are learning a new skill, take exams in the subject as these are excellent methods to gauge your new knowledge. Test out your new skill in as many different settings as possible. Teach this skill to others. This is probably the best indication of your new grasp on the subject.

Look to a mentor who has been successful in what you are trying to achieve. Mentoring is an important aspect of most success stories. A mentor can be anyone from an expert in a particular field offering training and his or her expertise to guide the apprentice towards excellence in the area, to the wise older person who can give life advice based on years of sometimes bitter experience. The inspiring words of a person who has fought the battles and triumphed over the struggles can motivate you to bring about necessary change.

Ask for feedback from others as to their opinion of your new success. Although you may not always receive the answer you want, adopting the right attitude to feedback should only make you work harder to achieve this goal.

ACTION SUMMARY

Goal-setting may be a very new exercise for you. You may initially see this practice as yet another burden in an already overburdened life. Who needs the extra hassle of setting and maintaining goals? The answer is – we all do.

CHAPTER 7

Out with the bad

Let's face it, at times life can suck. Sometimes we feel we're living out the saying, 'Often when the flowers arrive at the front door, the robber is leaving via the back door.'

Just when you think your problems or worries appear to be settling, some new dilemma starts, leaving you totally bewildered and imagining what next could possibly go wrong.

Because this never-ending pattern of ups and downs makes our existence so unpredictable, we have developed an entire series of coping mechanisms that allow us a temporary escape hatch throughout the day, week, month, year. There is not one person who does not have an escape in some shape or form.

Escape hatches can range from one's own personal quiet time to some horrible pharmacological addiction. The trick is to develop the escape hatch that doesn't plunge you into a much deeper hole.

I like to divide these hatches into a very succinct classification system: 'bad' or 'good'! Likewise, my formula for dealing with escape hatches: avoid the bad and nurture the good.

No doubt you are asking, 'What sort of fool does this guy take me for? This type of obvious stuff doesn't need to be spelt out.' Well, my answer to that comment is also very straightforward. If my formula is so obvious, then why do so many people continually perpetuate and choose the *bad* escape hatches?

Our bad escape hatches are:

1 anger
2 negativity
3 jealousy/envy
4 psychological or physical symptoms
5 addictions.

Let's look at each of them in turn.

1 ANGER

Most people don't see anger as anything other than a very negative form of loss of control, usually precipitated by something going wrong. You may be the cause of your own anger but in the majority of cases it is prompted by someone else.

Anatomically our brains are divided into different regions. Our basic bodily functions such as breathing, being awake, being asleep, hunger, bladder or bowel function are all mediated in the most primitive part of our brain known as the brainstem. Through training and socialisation we learn, to some extent, to wait for our meals and we avoid urinating on another person's foot just because our bladder is full. But as our basic urges are just that – basic – they don't require the sophistication of millions of coordinated sets of grey matter.

We then move up to the midbrain, which is like the relay station between primitive urges and controlled thought and emotion.

The neo-cortex is our conscious thinking brain, which can be divided into lobes or can also be considered as the left (analytical, linguistic, mathematical, concrete) brain and the right (creative, emotive, psychic) brain.

The lobes of the brain are the:

▸ frontal – social lobes
▸ parietal – sensory-motor lobes
▸ temporal – memory-emotive lobes
▸ occipital – visual areas.

This is a very gross division of a much more complex structure but is nonetheless reasonably accurate.

Hidden deep within the temporal lobes is an area called the amygdala. If I strapped you down to an operating table and placed a fine electrode into your brain right smack bang in the middle of the amygdala, and then hooked this little wire up to an electricity source, I could send even the most placid person into a rage.

Most of us don't need such extremes to feel anger. In fact (thankfully in a small minority) it doesn't take much at all to push some people into a serious rage. We've all witnessed the spectacle of a couple of lunatics almost coming to blows over a parking spot in a shopping centre. There must be something bizarre about a steering wheel, because quite a few people seem to 'fly off the handle' when they are in contact with these seemingly harmless pieces of hardware.

So there appears to be a number of human beings who seem to cope with misfortune by becoming angry. Why have I listed this as number one in the group of bad coping mechanisms? Because anger not only makes you quite obnoxious, it is not particularly good for your health.

Around 25 years ago, there was a big distinction between 'type A' and 'type B' personalities. The type A people were categorised as the driven, perfectionist, successful types and the type Bs were the lazy slobs with little motivation apart from an unhealthy desire to locate the remote control for the television.

The initial research on these two disparate groups suggested it was the type A personalities who suffered heart attacks much more

commonly than the type Bs. A few years later, after many of the
type A people had either suffered a heart attack through fear of suffering a heart attack, or had finally learnt to relax and perhaps even
sleep without their ties on, a more sensible researcher reanalysed
the data. The researcher discovered that it was a particular sub-
group of the type As who appeared to suffer most of the heart
attacks. Let's call them the type Cs.

These people had three important characteristics. They were:

▸ time-urgent
▸ negative
▸ angry and hostile.

Many studies have confirmed that within two hours of becoming acutely angry with anyone, you increase by 100 times your risk
of a heart attack.

I must remind you of that wonderful Buddhist statement, 'You
are not punished for your anger, you are punished by your anger.'

By the way, for all you non-angry, non-time-urgent but successful, driven, perfectionist type As, it has been found that if you have
a heart attack, your survival rates are much better than the type
Bs because you were much more diligent in controlling the
heart disease risk factors than the lazy, non-motivated type Bs who
couldn't be bothered changing lifestyles!

But back to our type Cs. You are basically a heart attack waiting
to happen. Well, what's the answer? The answer is very simple.
Don't get angry. You guessed it – I had to dig deep into the corridors
of my creativity to work out that little number!

Yes, by this stage, I'm sure all you disappointed angry types
have ripped this book to pieces in a fit of rage over the lack of reasonable guidelines. Don't worry, I will deal with these very specific guidelines when I discuss the last bad coping mechanism –
addictions – which needs very specific instructions. Suffice to say,
a five-step approach to changing bad coping mechanisms is
coming.

2 NEGATIVITY

So much has been said and written on optimists versus pessimists. If you are an optimist your glass is half full, if you are a pessimist, it's half empty. If you are a pessimist, anything that happens is bad luck and it will usually happen to you. I'm afraid I'm an optimist so it's difficult to give anything other than an optimist's perspective, which is very simple: positivity breeds positivity; negativity breeds negativity.

There are stories throughout the ages of very successful people, all of whom have been through negative periods in their lives. The old adage about good luck rings true: 'The harder I work, the luckier I become.' This principle is operative in all of our lives. There are so many people who are afflicted with enormous bad luck, disabilities or other misfortunes who can turn their lives around. Many of these people use misfortune to fuel their determination.

If you look for and take on board the negatives in life, they will just keep happening to justify your opinion. As I have said before, it is often the hardest life lessons that make us stronger and present us with opportunities for growth.

One of the most striking forms of negativity is our internal language. The more negative terms, phrases, words we bombard our brains with, the more negative situations will arise. The person who is constantly putting themselves down, using terms like 'you fool', 'you just aren't good at this', 'I hate myself', and so on, will find that they are uttering self-fulfilling prophecies.

If this is the language you use on yourself, imagine the manner in which you're perceived by other people. If you make a mistake, don't call yourself an idiot. Instead, say, 'That's okay – it's a learning experience. I won't make this mistake again.'

Colonel Sanders, in his late sixties, refused to accept a social security cheque. Instead he went from one chicken shop to the next, offering his secret recipe for fried chicken.

He had 1009 negative responses until one shop owner finally agreed to try the recipe. The rest is history. Likewise, as we saw in chapter 3, Thomas Edison failed many times before successfully inventing the light bulb. If these determined optimists had accepted the negative responses to their endeavours, we would still be fumbling around in the dark, not knowing what chicken we are eating!

No doubt at this point, the pessimists are thinking, you positive thinkers are just conning yourselves and you are in for a big fall when things go wrong. But if we all engage in negative thinking, all of us will feel worse when 'it' happens – if it does happen at all. And not only will we all feel worse, we won't have the positive resources to deal with a bad situation and turn it around.

See each challenge in life not as a negative but as a further opportunity for growth. Each new day is a new adventure. When we are awakened by our alarm clock, let's think of it now as an *opportunity* clock. See each difficult person you deal with during your day as an opportunity for you to refine your people skills. See each setback as a new intellectual challenge to make you a better problem-solver. The list goes on!

I'm not suggesting that every time something bad happens you say, 'Fantastic, I wish this happened to me all the time!' By all means, become upset when the situation demands it, but don't cling on to the situation.

I was the director of a cardiac assessment clinic using CT scanning of the coronary arteries to detect coronary artery calcium. This is an excellent, non-invasive method to detect early heart disease, so strategies can be implemented well before – at times decades before – the affected person would have suffered a heart attack.

This is, however, a controversial test because it is new. The conservative elements of medicine believe (of course I disagree) that as yet the evidence is not strong enough to justify using the test as a screening tool for heart disease.

This ongoing debate has meant a relatively constant barrage of criticism and misinformation from the conservatives and I must admit when I hear the negative comments I do not say, 'Oh, thank you for yet another learning experience.'

I get the expected knot in my stomach and feel acutely stressed.

But this is a short-lived reaction which I have learnt to turn around. Fortunately, when the dust of the acute reaction settles, I feel stronger.

I take great comfort in that wonderful saying, 'There has never been a monument erected to a critic.'

The reward for negativity is: negativity.

3 JEALOUSY/ENVY

'You've got something I don't have and I want it.' That basically sums up one of our most negative emotions. Jealousy can also involve possessiveness towards another person. Although there are times when jealousy can be considered reasonable and some would even say healthy under the circumstances, in most cases it does not serve the sufferer.

Of course, if our partner of fifteen years decides they would prefer another partner, most of us would be feeling the pangs of jealousy, regardless of our usual coping skills. In those circumstances, your response would be considered quite reasonable and expected. But often, when it happens it says more about your partner than you.

CASE STUDY – ROBERT

Robert Wilson is 42. He has a loving, supportive wife and two children aged fourteen and eight. Although his life at home was secure and fulfilled, he felt a constant need for new situations and challenges. He was an academic professor at a major university and was well respected for his work in the field of biochemistry. His lab was constantly publishing ground-breaking research and as recognition for his work, he was appointed head of the department at a rival campus.

Robert's dream for this extra power, status and recognition had become a reality. However, when anyone in society puts their head above the crowd, there are many people just waiting to knock it off.

For example, the associate professor in Robert's new department felt he was in line for Robert's position and although he was well aware of Robert's credentials, he had worked just as hard, giving years of loyal service to the university. It was his feeling that Robert's work was not as earth-shattering as implied by the general scientific community.

You can imagine the reception Robert received from this particular gentleman when he commenced his new position. This form of subtle professional jealousy can eat away at its perpetrator, destroying their effectiveness as a co-worker and person.

Another much more insidious problem, and certainly more far-reaching, came from a totally different quarter. Carolyn was an attractive 29-year-old single woman who worked as a research assistant in Robert's new lab. Carolyn had been involved with a number of men, usually 10 to 15 years older than her and usually in positions of power.

When Robert arrived at the lab, his striking appearance, blatant arrogant self-assuredness and obvious charisma was a magnet to a woman like Carolyn. To the outsider, her sycophantic behaviour from their first meeting would have been nauseating to observe, but to Robert this attractive young woman was yet another challenge to his ever increasing ego. He did not think of the disastrous consequences at many levels, from his professional life to the most important repercussions to his family.

The not-so-subtle overtures from Carolyn culminated in a passionate embrace when Robert and Carolyn were working late in the lab one night.

Although Robert didn't need this extra complication in his life, he foolishly did not resist her blatant advances and soon they were having an affair. As always, these clandestine activities were exposed, hurting innocent parties in the process.

Because these occurrences are so common it is important to understand their true nature. There is no doubt that some couples have lousy relationships and the progressive incompatibility can drive either partner into the arms of another person.

But what motivates a person who is in a very sound relationship to have an affair? In the case of males, I believe it is a combination of testosterone (the male hormone) and ego.

The male in a supportive, happy relationship usually has no intention of leaving his family. The Carolyns of this world (and I'm not suggesting they always have that specific name; please don't try to sue me) are purely sport. I believe this type of behaviour is a form of immaturity reflecting deep, unresolved intrapersonal problems.

The acute jealousy experienced by Robert's wife when the affair was discovered was a reasonable human emotion displayed by a person who had devoted years of love and support to a man who was often out furthering his own career instead of spending time at home.

The more pathological jealousy, however, was displayed by Carolyn. Robert's wife had everything she wanted and Carolyn would have done anything she could to extract it from her. Carolyn showed no regard for Robert or his family, seeing her attempt to win Robert as her right and only goal.

There are many psychopathological reasons for this type of behaviour. They usually extend back to early childhood relation-ships, as we discussed in chapter 4.

Robert's case demonstrates two very insidious but real forms of jealousy: professional jealousy and relationship jealousy.

Jealousy is a very bad coping mechanism that eats away at its owner. Most of us, given certain situations, have felt it acutely at different times. But the trick is to let go of the emotion as quickly as possible. In the next chapter, I will discuss the importance of forgiveness as a good coping mechanism. If you are jealous of someone else, or they are jealous of you and have wronged you because of it, discipline yourself to forgive.

Just like anger, you are not punished for your jealousy but by your jealousy.

4 PSYCHOLOGICAL OR PHYSICAL SYMPTOMS

External pressure of any type can promote any of the more overt bad coping mechanisms. Anger is usually pretty obvious, and you can sense when a person is negative almost from the moment they mope into the room. Anger can literally make you red in the face, and envy can show up there too. The cigarette smoker, the alcoholic or the drug addict are easy to pick. The bad coping mechanism that is not always obvious is when stress is internalised and changed into psychological or physical symptoms.

PSYCHOLOGICAL SYMPTOMS

The common psychological symptoms are:

(a) Anxiety
This commonly manifests as a general feeling of concern or worry precipitated by an event – minor or major. As we have seen in chapter 5, anxiety reactions are often accompanied by physical symptoms such as a sensation of an increase in the intensity and rate of the heartbeat (palpitations), sweating, a feeling of fullness in the head and often gastrointestinal symptoms ranging through loss of appetite, nausea, abdominal pain to diarrhoea and/or constipation. As already noted, these symptoms can be caused by stress, but they also may be evidence of serious underlying disease, so should always be investigated.

There are two basic psychiatric disorders: neuroses and psychoses. Neuroses are psychological manifestations in people who are still reasonably in touch with reality. Basically neuroses are accentuations of normal reactions. It is said that neurotics build castles in the air, psychotics live in them and psychiatrists collect the rent.

We all feel acutely anxious in dangerous or, at times, even

exciting situations. To feel anxious in a situation of minor danger, perhaps reliving an incident from years before, would be considered a neurotic reaction. I must point out that the perceived anxiety is real to the sufferer and should not be demeaned. This person needs expert help.

The famous psychiatrist Carl Jung once said, 'Neuroses are a psychological replacement for a more painful reality.'

Anxiety reactions which would be considered significant enough to be neuroses arise from deep in the psyche, usually as a result of incidents or traumas that occurred during childhood. Such incidents may be acutely traumatic, for example an attack by a dog on a small child, or a one-off episode of sexual abuse by an unknown attacker. Neuroses may also arise from longstanding psychological or physical abuse by an alleged carer or parent. These are the 'painful reality' referred to by Jung.

Other well-described neuroses, apart from a general feeling of anxiety, are as follows:

(b) Obsessive-compulsive neuroses

These usually manifest in the form of phobias (fear of heights, flying, spiders, snakes, tax collectors, and so on) or ritual behaviours such as repetitive hand-washing, checking the locks, the oven, etc., etc.

(c) Panic attacks

These are very serious forms of anxiety attacks that can be very disabling, often mimicking a severe physical problem such as a heart attack or severe angina.

(d) Agoraphobia

The person afflicted with this condition becomes acutely anxious when they leave the comforts of their own home.

(e) Hysteria

This most severe form of neurosis can present in many ways. Hysterical behaviour is sometimes manifested as a loss of function or feeling of one limb. Its most severe presentation is that of multiple personalities – as brought to popular attention in the movie *Sybil* starring Sally Field.

PHYSICAL SYMPTOMS

Unfortunately, as we have seen, many physical symptoms can be closely related to stress symptoms. Often there may be a minor phys- ical basis, but the stress markedly accentuates the symptoms. Stress symptoms can start at the top of your head at and work their way down to your toes. Anything from a wide variety of headaches to aches and pains in other areas of the body can be stress-related symptoms.

The common problems are as follows:

Headaches: Most of us have felt that tight band around our skull when we are becoming acutely stressed. In some people those headaches can occur on a daily basis, prompting some bright spark in the medical profession to call them chronic tension headaches – thank you, Einstein!

Migraines: These certainly have a strong physical and genetic basis but still occur more commonly when those predisposed are under stress.

Chronic stress can, however, lead to neck problems, which in turn can commonly contribute to recurrent headaches. In these days of computers, desk work and other sedentary jobs, the neck is often a factor and needs attention.

I saw a woman recently who, following a holiday in New Zealand, returned to work with a constant, daily headache. It would have been very easy to have attributed her symptoms to stress but on further questioning, I found she had been bungee jumping during her holiday and injured her neck unbeknownst to her. After appropriate neck exercises and remedial massage, her headaches promptly settled.

Cardiovascular symptoms: That poor old pulsating thing in your thorax, otherwise known as the heart, can certainly be the brunt of many stressful insults. I have already mentioned in chapter 1 the fear–flight/fight system and when this is switched on, all hell can break loose in the heart and its closely related arterial system. Anything like a pounding in your throat, chest or upper abdomen may signal an acute stress response, often in a completely normal heart. I couldn't begin to tell you the number of patients I have seen over the years with precisely this problem.

The major problem arises, however, when any significant life stress can precipitate a rapid heartbeat or a chest pain in a person with an underlying structural heart problem. As I have already mentioned, it can be quite dangerous to blame everything on stress and not thoroughly explore physical symptoms.

5 ADDICTIONS

The commonest and, in many ways, the worst escape hatch you can develop is an addiction to a drug.

Let's deal with these in order of statistical importance. Eighty per cent of drug-related deaths in our society are due to cigarette smoking. We won't look at the illegal drugs; they're not as readily available, so statistically, although they are just as deadly, they kill fewer people.

Unfortunately, around 20 per cent of any population carry strong receptors in their brain for nicotine addiction. This is why, despite all the health messages, around 25 per cent of the adult population continues to smoke. Nicotine addiction is a very powerful physical addiction. The effect of nicotine wears off within around half to one hour and therefore, if you're addicted, you start to feel the need for another cigarette within around one hour of the last.

It must really peeve someone who is truly addicted to nicotine to hear an ex-smoker say, 'I don't know what your problem is, I gave it up like that' as they sanctimoniously click their formerly nicotine-stained fingers.

The reality is, for those truly ingrained nicotine addicts, it ain't that simple. The source of their addiction is readily available, its effects wear off quickly, it still has borderline social acceptance in some circles and it does not cause obvious behavioural change or physical damage to the observer – unless they're unlucky enough to breathe in the stuff.

The insidious damage, however, is disastrous. As a cardiologist and consultant physician, I have witnessed all too often the profound damage to a person's health and the health of their family caused by long-term cigarette smoking.

CASE STUDY – JEANETTE

At the age of 38, Jeanette Macleod coughed blood. A chest X-ray and subsequent CT scan of the chest revealed a lung tumour and confirmed cancer at biopsy. She required an operation to remove her left lung.

Both her parents were smokers, a habit Jeanette commenced at age sixteen but, in reality, she had been smoking in some form for most of her life.

Her left lung was irradiated to ensure no trace of tumour remained and although there is disagreement in the medical world, I suspect her subsequent heart attack two years later was a combination of cigarette-induced coronary artery disease and irradiation-induced damage to her heart. The heart attack caused extensive damage and now at the age of 40, Jeanette is living with a heart that works at 30 per cent of its normal capacity and with one cigarette-damaged lung.

It is no wonder she becomes short of breath after even minimal activity – activity you and I would take for granted – such as walking upstairs, hurrying to catch a train or carrying shopping bags.

Stories like that of Jeanette shock and horrify non-smokers but still do not stop nicotine addicts from venturing into a tobacconist. Physical addictions are powerful motivators. They can be like little voices in your head saying, 'One won't hurt. Those doctors always exaggerate the damage. I had a chest X-ray which showed my lungs are perfect.' The most amazing comment I hear is, 'I'm not addicted, I just enjoy it!'

Let's analyse this statement. Just think logically about the physical act of enjoying putting a little white stick in your mouth, lighting the end with a match and sucking on the stick so you can inhale the smoke into your lungs. Give me a break! As a physical act, this cannot be enjoyable.

The only possible enjoyment can come from one of two aspects: addiction and ritual.

Addiction is easily the most prominent reason for smoking, and for claiming to enjoy it. When you're addicted to any substance and there are minimal amounts of that substance in your bloodstream, you crave that substance. Therefore the act of satisfying that addiction by introducing the substance into your body is enjoyable. The relief of any craving, therefore can be classified as enjoyable.

If you're a smoker, don't try to justify your addiction as some hedonistic act. At least be honest enough to admit you have an addiction. Once you make this declaration to yourself, you are in a more powerful position to make a decision to do one of two things: continue with your addiction and therefore accept the probable long-term consequences, or try to beat the addiction.

One of the major problems with nicotine addiction is that it usually starts in the teens. From the teens to the early twenties, most people think they are immortal and health issues are not usually a major concern. They assume they are healthy. If they carry enough nicotine receptors, those younger people who start smoking will quickly become addicted and become the very people who are long-term cigarette smokers, many of whom claim to enjoy smoking for enjoyment alone.

The second reason people claim to enjoy smoking is the enjoyment of the little rituals that have become ingrained with the habit.

CASE STUDY – PAM

Pam is 64 years old. She is an intelligent retired schoolteacher with well-controlled high blood pressure and a well-established cigarette habit that has lasted over 40 years. She also has a healthy desire to stop but really finds it hard to hit upon the winning formula. She is ostracised by her family and is sent outside to smoke.

'Where do you smoke?' I asked her.

She was rather bemused by my question.

'In the garden,' was her answer.

'Tell me more about the circumstances when you smoke,' I asked with some persistence.

Pam was now becoming more curious regarding my motives for pursuing this line of questioning, but she decided to humour me.

'I take the morning newspaper and sit in my favourite seat in a quiet place in the garden with a cup of coffee,' was her reply.

It doesn't take a genius to figure out that giving up cigarettes will be no easy task for Pam. Her brain has cleverly created a series of pleasurable, psychological associations to heighten her enjoyment of the act of smoking:

▸ She derives quiet time, by herself in a lovely setting in the garden, getting away from whatever stress may be happening in the house.
▸ She's sitting down in a favourite place.
▸ She sees this as a break, a form of relaxation.
▸ She is drinking a cup of coffee (another possible addiction).
▸ Finally, of course, her nicotine addiction is being satisfied.

WHY ADDICTIONS ARE SO HARD TO BREAK

Basically human beings at the 'animal level' are motivated by two things – the desire to seek pleasure and the need to avoid discomfort. This is no better demonstrated than in physical addictions.

With any physical addiction, we receive pleasure when our addiction is being satisfied and feel discomfort when the physical effects wear off. The power of physical addictions is such that young women will sell their bodies as prostitutes in order to feed their heroin habit. 'At least cigarettes aren't that bad,' the ingrained nicotine addicts might retort. But as we have seen, because they are legal and easily accessible, statistically cigarettes kill many more people than does heroin.

When I was doing my specialist training, I worked for a professor who had had coronary artery bypass surgery on two occasions, and who would advise patients all day not to smoke. At lunchtime, he would duck out the back of the building for a cigarette.

Despite the fact that this highly intelligent man knew cigarettes were potent killing machines and also knew their toxins had no doubt contributed to his severe heart disease, his addiction was so strong he continued to puff his life away (so to speak).

RIDDING YOURSELF OF BAD COPING MECHANISMS

The major behavioural strategy to rid yourself of any bad coping mechanisms is decision. You must decide what you want. If cigarettes, alcohol, heroin, cocaine, etc. are what you want, so be it. Just be very aware of the disastrous long-term consequences. If you want to continue to demonstrate anger, negativity and the other bad coping mechanisms we've discussed, that's your decision.

If, however, you decide that you – and that carbon-based life form you call your body – want to be healthy, live longer and develop more effective stress-relieving strategies, use the following Five-Step Action Plan.

5 STEP ACTION PLAN

1 Decide what you really want.
2 Interrupt your limiting pattern.
3 Create a new pattern.
4 Condition the new pattern with a plan and set of goals.
5 Live the program.

IMPLEMENTING THE FIVE-STEP ACTION PLAN

All forms of newly created behaviour come from the same basic neural (nerve) connections: thought–idea–decision–plan–action.

Our thoughts arise from our subconscious brain and are delivered to the conscious mind. If we then consciously attribute value to these thoughts, we crystallise them into an idea.

If there is appeal in this idea, which our inner being decides has value, we then translate that idea into a decision.

From the commitment to a decision we formulate a plan as to how best we can make this decision work for us. When this plan has been carefully formulated, we put the plan into action.

This is the universal pattern; our thoughts are powerful creators. Without our thoughts, there would be no tangible reality. Let's now look at each of the steps in our action plan to rid ourselves of bad coping mechanisms.

1 DECIDE WHAT YOU REALLY WANT

So many of us drift into particular life habits and patterns without really considering their consequences. Often a decision to change is precipitated by some dramatic life event such as the occurrence of a new symptom, the sudden death of a loved one or friend, or a major change in life direction.

In my heart clinic, I often see people who months earlier had heard me lecture at a conference about the benefits of a thorough preventative screen or of living a healthy lifestyle.

'Why has it taken you months to make an appointment?' I ask. The answer is almost always one of the following:

'I had an episode of chest pain last week.'

'My next-door neighbour died suddenly of a heart attack.'

'I resigned from my job a month ago and decided it's time to start thinking about my health.'

All excellent reasons for deciding on an assessment, but usually precipitated by an interruption in the usual life pattern.

Regardless of the trigger, the first step in changing a bad coping mechanism is making the decision to change. And an important facet of decision-making is goal-setting.

Specific goals with specific aims and time frames (such as short, medium and long-term) are excellent methods for reinforcing your decisions. I've covered goal-setting in detail in chapter 6, so turn to that chapter for the good oil on how to incorporate goal-setting into your life. One invaluable tool that I'd like to remind you of here is the Life Journal.

In your Life Journal, have a specific area for life goals, which obviously flow from your decisions. Remember goals (which can be defined as dreams with a specific time frame) cannot be implemented without the initial decision to create them in the first place.

2 INTERRUPT YOUR LIMITING PATTERN

Once you have made the decision as to what you really want and have set achievable goals that will allow you to implement your decision, then you must examine what limiting patterns are standing in your way.

Without wishing to seem like I have a vendetta against cigarette smokers, the limiting patterns that are involved with this addiction are excellent case illustrations for discussion.

There are, of course, five aspects of limiting patterns that need to be examined when considering the bad coping mechanisms highlighted by addiction:

- (a) rituals
- (b) addictive behaviour and effects (including withdrawal symptoms)
- (c) 'roadblocks'
- (d) high-risk behaviour
- (e) pleasure–pain reversal.

(a) RITUALS

For the cigarette smoker, the little rituals – such as we saw in the case study of Pam with the coffee, the newspaper, the garden and the cigarette in solitude – markedly reinforce the reliance on bad coping mechanisms.

Some people have a favourite chair, a particular time such as when the phone rings, or even just the break from work to leave the premises to stand outside in the elements and puff away, either lost in your own thoughts or sharing the smoke-filled air with your fellow nicotine addicts.

These rituals become part of the physically addicted's way of life. Just the thought of them can squirt a few more endorphins and some dopamine into the bloodstream, making the breaking of the habit that much harder.

(b) ADDICTIVE BEHAVIOUR AND EFFECTS

As I have stated, around 20 per cent of people have strong receptors in their brains for nicotine addiction. Once these receptors have been introduced to nicotine, it is rapidly incorporated into normal day-to-day cell metabolism. Without the nicotine running around in your bloodstream, you feel very uncomfortable. The brain then starts to send little messages, such as, 'Come on, just one more – it's not that bad, think how you feel without nicotine, you could be knocked over by a bus,' etc.

The irritability starts, and mood swings and even depression can set in without nicotine in the system. Probably (psychology aside), the greatest limiting pattern for the nicotine addict is weight gain. I've already discussed in chapter 6 the reasons for this phenomenon, but I'll reiterate here that when you stop smoking (difficult enough, I know) it is also important to maintain a calorie-restricted diet and an exercise program, to ensure you do not gain weight.

The symptoms of withdrawal from alcohol and illegal drugs are even more profound and debilitating than those from cigarettes. As I said at the beginning of this chapter, it is certainly much better not to start these bad coping mechanisms in the first place.

(c) ROADBLOCKS

Dr Vic Strecher, from Ann Arbor University in Michigan, is the world expert on 'health tailoring'. Doctor Strecher is endeavouring to bring the health professions forward to a point that the retailing world reached years ago.

In retail, it is definitely not 'one size fits all'. Doctor Strecher's view is that in health prevention we should similarly be tailoring our messages to suit each individual's needs.

What may work for one person certainly may have no effect for another. During my time as a medical student, I saw numerous examples of lives that had been destroyed by cigarettes either through emphysema or cancer.

These scarred, black, horrible ex-sponges that at one stage attempted to shift air in and out with each laboured breath should turn anyone off smoking. Using these examples as horror tactics, however, does not work for everyone.

Addiction – to any pharmacological substance – can be so strong that shock strategies are of limited value. As I have stated, the brain creates a series of subconscious cues to reinforce the pleasure of smoking or of ingesting any other substance the body craves.

When dealing with addictions, there is another factor that also happens to get in the way. This is a little thing called life, which throws up what Dr Strecher calls roadblocks. These are the situations that make travelling along the path to ridding ourselves of these bad coping mechanisms so much more difficult.

The obvious example is the subject of this book – stress! Any life stress can make the motivation and desire to stop smoking so much more difficult. And stress and addiction are closely intertwined. Our brain has several distinct though connected centres, each dependent on the other in a wonderfully synergistic fashion. We have a centre for stress that fires off the usual reaction when stress occurs.

Well, our stress centre is rather close to our addiction centre and when one is stimulated, the other starts firing in sympathy. So, when you're stressed for any reason your addiction centre goes along for the ride. The more you are stressed, the more you want your addiction satisfied.

Then, when your addiction is temporarily alleviated, you feel comparatively less stressed. But when a cigarette smoker is stressed, that hit of nicotine will make them feel better for a short period of time only. Therefore, especially when you're under periods of greater stress, trying to stop cigarettes is not easy.

A second major roadblock to stopping your addiction is association with other addicts. The heroin culture is a classic example. To obtain this illegal drug, you must associate with a subculture of people who use and sell the stuff. The more you associate with these people, the harder it is to extricate yourself from this world in order to detoxify. In a bizarre and destructive way, these people become your social support.

Living with another smoker is, of course, a major roadblock to giving up the legal evil weed. Unless both parties are committed, it becomes very difficult for either to stop.

Whatever the addiction, I'm confident that those with this problem can list a series of reasons why giving up is very difficult. Regardless, making the decision and recognising the obstacles to change are the most important initial steps towards successfully breaking that addiction.

(d) HIGH-RISK BEHAVIOUR

You can consider roadblocks as external pressures that prevent you from quitting your addiction. There are, however, a series of internal behavioural patterns that also limit our ability to maintain our strength of purpose. Probably the best example of high-risk behaviour is the use of other drugs. If you're trying to stop smoking, the Friday night sojourn to the local hotel for drinks with your friends will be a disaster. After a few drinks, one of your so-called friends will offer you a cigarette – despite the fact you may have been strong for a few days – and now you're back on the habit.

The use of any illegal drugs also accentuates your use of legal drugs such as cigarettes and alcohol.

CASE STUDY – KIM

Kim Napier was 31 years old. She had two children aged four and eight. She was an ex-heroin addict, a habit she'd kicked three years before. Two habits she couldn't kick were cigarettes and alcohol. These drugs were much cheaper and easier for her to obtain.

Kim could not walk past a liquor store without purchasing alcohol. She first came under my care when she was admitted to hospital with a severe infection on one of her legs. This infection, known as cellulitis, cleared with high doses of intravenous antibiotics, withdrawal from alcohol and a few days' rest in hospital.

The father of Kim's children had long since moved on, leaving Kim's long-suffering aunty to care for them during Kim's multiple illnesses.

Kim's leg infections recurred and unfortunately due to the hepatitis B and C she contracted during her years as a heroin addict, she developed severe cirrhosis of the liver. Her liver was scarred from the constant pounding from alcohol on an already inflamed organ.

Kim required multiple admissions to hospital and with each bout of leg infection and each drinking bout, her condition deteriorated. She continued to smoke 60 cigarettes per day, which also affected her general health.

One very unfortunate day – despite the hours of counselling, social support and the previous personal commitments from Kim that she would stop drinking if only for her children's sake – she was admitted to hospital in a coma.

The coma was due to liver failure precipitated by a severe gastrointestinal bleed. Kim died three days later, leaving her two small children without any parents at all.

Kim's wasted life was basically the result of perpetual high-risk behaviour. So if you are committed to stopping your addiction, you must recognise your own high-risk behaviours and try your best to stop them.

You may have to change your social outlets for a while or, in the case of very damaging relationships, permanently. A new group of friends may be just the solution to turn around these bad behavioural patterns.

(e) Pleasure–pain reversal

As I have mentioned, there is no doubt when you analyse every human act at its basic core, it is either due to the desire to seek pleasure or the desire to avoid discomfort. The pleasure – perceived or real – derived from an addiction makes it difficult to walk away from permanently, especially when you are met by the aforementioned roadblocks or continue to engage in high-risk behaviour.

Addictions are reinforced by what I refer to as pleasure–pain reversal. This concept was pioneered by the founders of neuro-linguistic programming, better known as NLP.

Whatever bad coping mechanisms we have established as prominent life patterns are reinforced in our brain by associating them with pleasure.

Our brains also associate discomfort with the withdrawal of any of our bad coping mechanisms. Thus we are locked into this behaviour. If you are truly serious about a permanent change of this behaviour, the pleasure–pain cycle must be reversed.

CASE STUDY – CON

Con Marcos is a 33-year-old builder with two small children. He smoked 30 cigarettes per day and had tried to stop on a few occasions.

'But I love smoking,' he said to me during our initial consultation. 'I really hang out for smoko every day, it's a great break from the day-to-day hassles of work!'

On further discussion, I discovered his father had died at the age of 45 of an acute heart attack, when Con was only fourteen.

'How did you feel at your dad's funeral?' I asked a bemused Con.

'It was the worst day of my life,' he replied with a slight wince.

'How many children do you have, Con?' I asked.

'Two.'

'What are their ages?' I persisted.

'Six and nine.'

'Now, Con, you're going to think I'm being rather nasty here, but I know you are serious about stopping smoking. Every time you feel like smoking a cigarette, I want you to develop a vivid picture in your mind of a church. I want you to imagine this church in great detail: the colour, the sound of the organ playing, the solemn looks on the faces of the congregation.

'In this church, imagine a coffin. In the front row of the church sit your wife and your two small children with tears pouring down their faces, staring at your coffin. I want you to remember the pain you felt at your father's funeral and truly imagine your wife and children feeling that same pain at your funeral. You must vividly visualise this scene each and every time you feel like a cigarette.'

Con sat there stunned as he realised the very dramatic point I was making. But, if he was serious about making a dramatic and drastic change in his behaviour, he needed to take dramatic and drastic measures.

Only you know what prompt will be effective for you to make these dramatic changes, so take some time now to decide what will work for you and put this into action.

For the most effective achievement of pleasure–pain reversal, adopt the following plan:

(i)   Decide what bad coping mechanism you wish to change.
(ii) Associate enormous pain with this coping mechanism.
(iii) Link an unrelated pleasure with avoidance of the bad coping mechanism.
(iv) Select an appropriate time in your life, preferably when roadblocks and high-risk behaviours are exerting minimal impact.
(v)   Start intense and reinforced practice of the pleasure–pain reversal.

There are a few key caveats. When I say 'link an unrelated pleasure', I'm not suggesting you replace one bad coping mechanism with another. For example, I am not suggesting you should stop smoking and replace it with overeating as a reward for not smoking. I'm suggesting you should use little tricks like psychological rewards. Tell yourself, 'I've gone an extra hour without a cigarette – how strong am I' and so on.

Secondly, there are times in all our lives when trying to rid ourselves of our bad coping mechanisms will not work. Don't try to stop smoking during a divorce or through your child's detoxification from heroin. You are basically just adding another stress to your already overloaded life.

Try also not to do this alone. You would not be expected to train for the Olympics without a coach: why then would anyone expect you to take such an important step alone? Seek help from an expert. Make open declarations to your friends and loved ones about what you are going to achieve. The more public your efforts in trying to change your bad coping mechanisms, the more chance you have of success.

Finally, don't throw in the towel. If your first few attempts don't succeed, keep trying. To change an ingrained bad behaviour, especially if it involves a pharmacological addiction, is not easy and often takes a few attempts. If you really want to, you will eventually succeed.

3 CREATE A NEW PATTERN

Whether your addiction is nicotine, alcohol, heroin or one of many other harmful substances (not to mention excessive food), obtaining and using this substance becomes a prominent part of your life.

Your brain becomes geared towards the rituals, behaviours and associations you have created which involve this bad coping mechanism. There is wonderful old saying, 'If you squeeze an orange you get orange juice.' Or in other words, if you stress a person you really find out what is inside them.

If you switch off your computer and then switch it back on, the default mechanism kicks in, delivering you to the programs in their initial state. If you have a longstanding, ingrained behaviour and you do not reprogram yourself, every time you are confronted with a situation involving this behaviour, your default mechanism will switch on.

This is a normal human response which allows us to perform a series of semi-automatic acts without having to waste enormous cerebral energy. The problem arises when these default behaviours induce long-term physical, mental or emotional harm in ourselves or our loved ones.

Don't be fooled into thinking you can switch off this behaviour at will. You have to formulate a plan and train a new behaviour and this is not easy. I have already given you the tools which will enable you to break these patterns, but you must also replace them with an entirely new pattern.

To create this new pattern, I suggest the following five-point plan:

- **(a)** state your goal
- **(b)** use planning
- **(c)** make the new pattern attractive
- **(d)** make the new pattern creative and novel
- **(e)** make the new pattern realistic and sustainable.

(a) STATE YOUR GOAL

In your Life Journal (which I discussed in chapter 6 in relation to goal-setting) write down the heading 'New pattern'.

You then must clearly, simply and concisely state the new pattern, in the present tense. For example:

- ▸ I am a non-smoker.
- ▸ I do not smoke.
- ▸ I respect my body and therefore, every day, practise healthy lifestyle principles.

Although more long-winded, this last statement is the most powerful because it is the most positive, affirmative message to your subconscious.

It is important to re-read your goal statements and every day, when you are alone, reaffirm these statements. A powerful technique is to sit alone in a quiet environment and repeat these statements out loud. The subconscious mind does not use the same logical principles which dictate the workings of our conscious mind. Therefore, the constant repetition of statements, either positive or negative, will be taken on board by the subconscious and eventually will become reality.

Basically, from the day we're born, the messages we choose to believe will then determine how we behave. If the messages you allow to filter to your subconscious are positive, then you become a positive person. If you learn to filter out the negative messages and incorporate the positive messages, you will then magically witness a flow of positive attitudes and subsequent positive occurrences in your life – you'll begin to feel the Life Factor in action.

Sure, there will be times in your life when bad things happen. But it is my belief that when you practise constant repetition of positive goals and statements, you will begin to view even negative occurrences as opportunities for further growth.

Therefore, set your definite, positive goals. Write them down, read them daily and reinforce them by constant repetition.

(b) Use planning

A goal is the key that unlocks the gateway to a new behaviour, but you must also have a definite plan to allow your goals to become a reality.

A truly intelligent person asks many questions. In my field of cardiology there is often a rather mechanical approach taken to a person's problems.

CASE STUDY – RODNEY

Rodney Cane is a 53-year-old property developer. At the age of 39 he had his first coronary artery bypass procedure and underwent a repeat operation at age 45. Three years later, he suffered further angina, finding it hard to take out his garbage bins. Any minimal activity would precipitate his angina.

The problem for Rodney is that his doctors did not ask the obvious question: why does this man have such premature, aggressive, recurring heart disease? Once this question is answered, then a plan can be set in place to address this vital issue.

Seeing Rodney's case as a pure mechanical problem creates purely mechanical solutions. Therefore when he develops the blockage, the solution is to open up the blockage with either surgery or a stent. This procedure is, of course, valuable in acutely treating a potentially fatal blockage but does not address the underlying cause.

Rudyard Kipling summarised intelligent questioning beautifully with the following verse: 'I have six faithful serving men for everything I do; their names are what and why and when and how and where and who.'

So, when confronted with a problem or when you have a goal, begin to formulate your plan with a series of questions. If your goal is to stop smoking, then ask the following questions:

▸ What will I achieve by stopping smoking?
▸ Why do I need to stop?
▸ Where should I seek guidance?
▸ When should I start?
▸ Who will benefit by my stopping smoking?

Some of these questions overlap, but they all achieve the goal of formulating a plan.

Here's another example: say you are starting to notice (much to your dismay) that your waistline is beginning to bulge. Your decision is obvious. You want to lose weight! But we all know it's not that simple.

Break down the issue into its component parts. Ask and answer the following five questions regarding your weight:

▸ What type of food do I eat and are there any particular foods that I know are contributing to my weight gain?
▸ How much food am I eating during the day and by how much am I prepared to cut this back?
▸ When am I eating – do I divide my eating throughout the day or mainly have one large meal?
▸ Who am I – do I come from a family prone to overweight and obesity-related health issues?
▸ Why do I overeat (if indeed you do)? Is it for comfort, for social reasons, or for pure hedonistic pleasure?

Use the what, why, when, how, where and who to break up any particular habit into its component parts.

Don't stop there! Learn as much as you can about the facts behind and around your habits and learn about creating new, more empowering behaviours. Read books, listen to audio tapes or CDs whilst driving, attend seminars, speak to experts, have a coach or mentor. Take positive steps every day to educate yourself about the entire subject. This, in itself, will reinforce in your mind the need for change. If you know more, you will be able to bring about the necessary change.

Mind you, you can formulate as many questions as you like using these 'faithful serving men' but, as with all plans, keep it simple.

So, your five-point plan to create a new pattern will involve:

▸ asking the right questions
▸ seeking the appropriate people to help you create this new pattern

▸ setting a firm date to put into action your new plan
▸ writing down a complete list of the benefits (for example, health, financial, social)
▸ working out the best strategies (with help) that can assist you in creating this new pattern.

(C) MAKE THE NEW PATTERN ATTRACTIVE

For a new pattern or behaviour to be successful, it must be attractive to you in the first place. This is why the pleasure–pain principle is so important. I have often seen patients under my care stop smoking following a heart attack. The initial pain is so bad that the person gives up cigarettes. Occasionally, however, as the months roll on and the stresses return with a vengeance, the urge to suck on a cigarette returns and during a moment of weakness, the addiction kicks back in.

This is why the pleasure side of the equation is important. Make sure your new pattern is not just because of the negative consequences of the old behaviour but is also associated with the positive, appealing consequences of the new behaviour.

In the case of giving up smoking, accentuate the financial gain, the clearer lungs, the personal achievements and inner strength you're displaying – the list goes on.

In your Life Journal, write down an unstructured list of any behaviour that you know is not harmful and you are happy to continue.

This can be anything from reading a crime novel to enjoying a good cup of espresso coffee. Once you have exhausted your list, think of a creative way you can associate your new behaviour with these old, enjoyable behaviours.

Linking these behaviours reinforces the enjoyment and ensures the success of your desired change.

(d) MAKE THE NEW PATTERN CREATIVE AND NOVEL

All human beings crave novelty. Constant repetition, although important in many aspects of our life, nevertheless can create boredom and lack of interest. Thus to make a new pattern more successful, new and creative techniques are an important tool. Your new pattern should be just that – new!

To give you a few examples, if you kick any addiction, there is always a strong financial gain.

Begin planning immediately, with the very first dollar of the money that once supported your addiction. Plan to save the money for the holiday that previously you could never afford. For example, if you spent $50 per week on your cigarette habit, that becomes around $2,500 over one year. This alone contributes very nicely to an airfare or accommodation in an upmarket resort.

Develop a vivid picture of you sunbaking on a secluded beach in the South Pacific with warm tropical air, dazzling white sand and turquoise water. All because you had the strength to rid yourself of a habit that was destroying your health.

The more vivid and realistic you can make this creative goal, the more effective you will be at ridding yourself of your bad coping mechanism.

Holidays do not have to be your focus. Stopping your addiction may allow you to purchase a new item for your house, enjoy a weekly outing with your loved ones, afford a new hobby – the possibilities are endless. You're only limited by the power of your imagination. Vividly imagine your lungs being cleared of that horrible tar or your liver regenerating once you stop drinking.

I would suggest you spend around 5 to 10 minutes every day visualising the damaged areas of your body healing. You'll find a detailed discussion about the techniques and benefits of visualisation in chapter 6.

(e) MAKE THE NEW PATTERN REALISTIC AND SUSTAINABLE

All the techniques already mentioned will help you to make this new pattern sustainable. Your goals should, therefore, be realistic. If you have tried to give up cigarettes 'cold turkey' and failed miserably, try another approach. It is not realistic just to say, 'I'm going to quit tomorrow.'

A carefully planned, simple strategy with clear, concise written goals in your Life Journal will make your goal easier to attain. But remember, you must commit yourself to regular practice of this plan or it cannot be sustained.

4 CONDITION THE NEW PATTERN

Now that you have firmly established your new pattern with clear and specific goals to achieve your desired outcome, it is vital that this pattern becomes a normal part of your everyday life.

This new pattern replaces your old, bad coping mechanism and, just like the old mechanism, it should become habitual. For anything to become habitual it must be performed daily for at least one month.

Therefore, for you to be successful at conditioning this new pattern, you should follow these five principles:

- **(a)** discipline
- **(b)** ritual
- **(c)** anticipation
- **(d)** simplicity
- **(e)** habit.

(a) DISCIPLINE

It is usually easier for us to avoid a new behaviour than practise it.

One of the fascinating questions in human behaviour is: what makes two people with similar skills and intelligence so vastly different in their life outcomes? Why would one person be a winner, always seeming to achieve his or her desired goals, and the other person, with seemingly similar skill levels, constantly fail? The true answer is discipline. Discipline is the key to being able to condition your new pattern.

(b) RITUAL

Use your discipline to make your new pattern a daily ritual. Set aside a particular time every day for meditation, visualisation, exercise or whatever you have decided your new pattern will be. Associate your new behaviour with activities such as meditation sessions, relaxation therapy, a remedial massage, nature, or beautiful relaxing music. It's all about carefully planning what you really want.

(c) ANTICIPATION

Make this pattern something you look forward to. Don't see it as a chore.

CASE STUDY – ALISON

One of my dear old patients, Alison, was 88 years old and had a significant heart condition. She needed to lose some weight but found walking quite a burden. We formulated a simple plan to develop her new behaviour.

She loved the 'daytime soapies'. Every afternoon she would sit in front of the television, starting with *Days of Our Lives* and finishing with *The Young and the Useless* – sorry, *Restless* – and spend time engrossed in her two shows. My suggestion was that she purchase a second-hand exercise bike and put it in front of the television.

Alison developed the new association that every time she visited the television room to watch her beloved soapies, instead of sitting on the lounge, she would sit on the exercise bike and gently pedal.

She proudly informed me that she pedalled 20 kilometres per day, five days per week (as the soapies aren't on over the weekend). Not bad for an 88-year-old woman!

This brings up a vital point – association. If you want to reinforce a new behaviour, associate it with an old, pleasurable behaviour. What you select is, of course, your business. Only you know what you find enjoyable and what turns you off.

(d) SIMPLICITY

Try to make your new pattern uncomplicated. The human condition enjoys simplicity. Therefore keep it simple!

(e) HABIT

Remember the one-month rule. Discipline yourself to stick to your new pattern for one month. After that, it is easy and becomes part of your normal daily habits.

5 LIVE THE PROGRAM

Once the pattern is conditioned, it is reinforced every time you repeat and practise. It will only be of benefit when you perform it.

I remember being astounded when a patient said to me, 'I couldn't possibly have a heart problem, I used to be an Olympic athlete.' This overweight ex-warrior was under the delusion that his behaviour of twenty years ago could offer protection in his current situation. Nothing could be further from the truth.

For any behaviour to have benefit, it must be continued, usually on a daily basis. Regular dieting or exercise will have lifelong benefit if it is continued indefinitely. The benefits are lost within weeks or months after reverting to old behaviours.

The more a new practice is reinforced, the more it will become habitual and therefore easier to perform. Although we crave novelty, many aspects of our psyche need stability. Daily routines are part of that stability. An activity that initially seemed difficult to sustain can be transformed, through regular practice, into a daily routine that we find we cannot do without.

Although I love sport, I personally do not derive any real pleasure from jogging. If, however, you ask regular joggers, they will almost universally tell you they look forward to their daily exercise and feel cheated if something prevents them from doing it.

They are almost addicted to the exercise and need their daily hit. In fact, many forms of exercise release endorphins, the brain's natural opiates. So the notion of addiction to exercise is not just psychological.

ACTION SUMMARY

Only you can make the decision to rid yourself of bad coping mechanisms. Using the strategies I have outlined, you can decide to interrupt your old limiting behaviours and addictions, create a new pattern and incorporate it into your life. Most importantly, live the program! Basically this Five-Step Action Plan can be used for all bad coping mechanisms. Life is, in reality, a mind game where you are the ultimate decision-maker. You decide how you will react to any situation, dilemma, good fortune or bad fortune that is presented to you.

Success in all aspects of life is yours if you want it. You just have to want it enough.

CHAPTER 8

In with the good

Nature abhors a vacuum. Therefore, if after reading chapter 7 you have made a decision and followed through with this decision to rid yourself of bad coping mechanisms, these need to be replaced with something else. This is where the good coping mechanisms come into play.

The good coping mechanisms Five-Step Action Plan is as follows:

1 Deal with acute stress.
2 Make the most of your time.
3 Declutter your life.
4 Be positive and maintain a sense of humour.
5 Create balance in your life through self-development and self-care.

1 DEAL WITH ACUTE STRESS

Unless you shut yourself away from the world and have close to no human contact, there is not much doubt that some form of stress will catch up with you. I'm bold enough to suggest it is unavoidable in modern society.

You can read as many motivational books, attend stress management courses or meditate until you are serene in the face but, when that stress happens, it still makes you feel lousy. How it manifests itself in your case is purely your decision. As we have seen, it may cause all manner of psychological or physical symptoms, make you plunge further into the legal or illegal addiction of your choice, or even worse prompt you to inflict psychological or physical harm on the people around you.

We've looked at ways to rid ourselves of those bad coping mechanisms for dealing with stress. But there's no doubt that we'll still be confronted with acute episodes of stress, which can threaten our hard-won new patterns and behaviours. So, do you continue to be plagued by acute stress or is there an approach you can adopt? The answer, you probably won't be surprised to find out, comes in the following five-point approach to dealing with acute stress:

(a) allow the acute reaction
(b) confront the stress
(c) start action to deal with the stress
(d) five stages of grief
(e) turn stress around.

(a) ALLOW THE ACUTE REACTION

When you feel stressed, irritated, annoyed by something going wrong in your life, guess what – it's normal! There is absolutely nothing wrong with this feeling and if you didn't allow yourself to have these allegedly negative feelings, I would suggest there would be something wrong with you.

If, for example, you lose your job, experience the death of a loved one, or make a dreadful mistake – especially when this impacts on other people – you will feel stressed.

The Reverend Lionel Thomas turned up one day for an appointment. When I greeted him in the waiting room, I was not met with his usual cheery disposition. The conversation was stilted during the walk down the corridor to my office. It didn't take much intuition to realise something had gone horribly wrong in his life.

When we sat opposite each other across my desk, I looked him squarely in his obviously bloodshot eyes and asked him what had gone wrong. Tears appeared in the corners of his eyes as he informed me his wife had died one month before.

I did not beat around the bush. I said to him, 'You must be feeling horrible. There's nothing worse that could happen to you and if you get over it, it will take you months.'

He then confessed to me how empty he felt, not just over his wife's death, but also because in many ways his feelings over her death had made a mockery of the pathetic platitudes he had dished out to other people he had ministered to during his many years as a clergyman.

My declaration allowed him to feel some relief at having his feelings validated. I had given him 'permission' to feel bad, lonely and abandoned. I basically said that was how he should feel and it was okay.

When he returned to see me a few months later, he was much happier. He will never recover from the death of his wife but time has, to a great extent, healed his wounds. He told me at that consultation that it was his initial conversation with me during his acute grief that was the start of his recovery.

In many ways, just to realise that it's all right to feel bad when confronted with acute stress is the first step in dealing with the stress.

(b) CONFRONT THE STRESS

Once a stressful event or situation has arisen in your life, your conscious and subconscious brain has registered the stress and you respond accordingly. As your subconscious cannot tell the differ-ence between fact and fantasy, until you confront and deal with the stress, your body will still experience a reaction to the stress.

To suppress the stress will have no benefit. It must be confronted.

An important piece of advice prior to you confronting this stress at a purely emotional level and possibly committing an act you may later regret, is to write out the key points on a large piece of paper. Obviously this technique depends on the situation. If the acute stress consists of your being robbed or assaulted, you can't very well ask your attackers if they have pen and paper. But if in your view you have been wronged by another person and you have time to consider how best you can react, putting your thoughts to paper can have powerful effects.

Discussing the situation as soon as possible with a confidant or even a trained counsellor may help you put the entire situation into perspective.

Some people prefer direct confrontation with the perpetrator and although eventually this is the final solution, I believe it is better to allow your acute reactions to settle if possible.

The worst approach is to allow the stress to occur and then attempt to 'sweep it under the carpet'.

If I am stressed about any particular matter, I usually will wake in the early hours of the morning and formulate my reply/retort to the perpetrator of that stress. Until I extract myself from a warm bed, stumble my way to the study and write out my thoughts, I find it hard to drift back to sleep.

After the preparation of my reply, I feel much better and my sub-conscious then allows me to return to a more peaceful slumber. This may not be your idea of a good time (frankly, it's not mine either) but the point I'm making is that some part of your brain will not allow you to ignore a significant stress once it has occurred.

Whether part of your acute response is to talk, write, think, or even engage in a less productive activity, the two behaviours I would strongly counsel you against are reacting in anger or conversely attempting to suppress the stress.

(c) START ACTION TO DEAL WITH THE STRESS

Thank God we are all different! One of my major failings is my inability to confront people. I would prefer to follow as many lines of diplomacy as are available to me rather than engage in brutally honest confrontation.

Although there is a time and place for both diplomacy and confrontation, the advantage of the acute, honest confrontation is that it short-circuits prolonged, brooding resentment. Sure, you risk becoming acutely unpopular (which isn't fun, I know) but at least it is out in the open and finished.

I'm working hard on this obvious flaw in my character. I do, however, find that disciplining myself to sit down and write the letter I discussed in the last section is the first step in the process of dealing with acute stress.

See any acute stress, once your initial reaction has settled, as you would any goal or issue in your life. Use chapter 6, which discusses goal-setting and action strategies, to help you formulate a plan to deal with the stress.

The technique of visualisation (also discussed in chapter 6) is particularly useful. Once you have clearly identified the issues involved in the particular stressful situation, use the following visualisation steps.

- Visualise (sit alone with eyes closed) a meeting with the people involved.
- Visualise a frank discussion of the issues, clearly putting forward your viewpoint but also trying to understand the other party's position.
- Visualise a positive outcome, beneficial to both sides.

Remember, no matter how much you have been wronged, forgiveness and moving on is always the best policy. Revenge has never solved anything.

How many people, including innocent parties like children, do you know whose lives have been destroyed by prolonged litigation, never-ending disputes with families or neighbours or even the chronic stress of staying in a job they can't stand? So, when you decide to take action to start dealing with whatever stress has occurred, ensure this action is motivated by the best intentions for a positive outcome for all parties in the long term.

This doesn't mean that as imperfect human beings we can be confronted with an acute stress and feel grateful it has happened, but once the stress has occurred and we have dealt with our acute reactions, we can develop plans and strategies to deal with the problem.

(d) FIVE STAGES OF GRIEF

In many ways, acute stress (and for that matter, chronic stress as well) is a form of loss. This loss is usually the loss of control of a situation. You have no control over the death of a loved one, infidelity by your partner, the reactions of those around you or bad luck, such as accidents.

As I mentioned earlier, Elizabeth Kubler-Ross first introduced the concept of the five stages of grief. Her focus mainly concerned the stages experienced by someone confronting their own death. But the stages she identified are relevant to any grief, loss or stress response. The stages are as follows:

(i) Anger
This is a typical response to acute stress. Although anger is very difficult to control and is a common, initial response in most of us, it is the degree of anger that is the real problem.

Unfortunately, some people overreact in this stage. At its extreme, anger can result in violent acts that are always regretted. If you're a person prone to uncontrollable loss of temper, don't wait until you induce grievous bodily harm on another human being; seek help now.

As for any problem, the first step towards recovery is recognising you have a problem. I believe that just like addictions excessive anger needs a full, professionally supervised program of management.

(ii) Denial

Trying to sweep stress under the carpet may give you temporary relief, but in the long term it solves nothing. There is, however, emotional logic in acutely denying a stress, purely to allow the acute emotions to simmer until you are in a better position to start the healing process.

So, a short period of denial may be useful and probably will occur at some early stage of coping with an acute stress.

(iii) Bargaining

It is very typical for us humans to try to bargain our way into a better position. 'Haggling' is an art form in the markets of Asia and will certainly occur in your mind at some stage during the acute stress response.

During a protracted, bitter divorce, this bargaining is known by the more formally accepted name of 'negotiation'. Bargaining your way to a better position can have some healing effects as well.

An obvious form of bargaining can often be seen in the self-talk people use after the break-up of a relationship. 'I'll have more time for myself', 'I'll be able to go on that holiday' and so on.

(iv) Depression

Sadness, acute grief or just plain unhappiness is a very common response to acute stress. When something bad happens to you, you should feel sad. As we saw in the case of Reverend Thomas earlier in this chapter, it is not a sign of weakness on your part, it is normal.

Don't let anyone who is not experiencing the stress make you feel bad about your reaction. Unfortunately, there are too many people out there who think they're doing the right thing by telling you to 'be strong', 'pull yourself together', 'there are plenty of fish in the sea', 'you'll get over it' and whatever other platitudes they can trot out.

It's okay to feel bad for a period of time after an acute stress or to feel bad on a regular basis during chronic stress. But, feeling bad is not an excuse for inaction in relation to the stress.

(v) *Acceptance*

This is the final stage of the acute reaction and the most rewarding. If your lifelong partner has died, if there was deep love between the two of you, you'll probably never completely get over the death – and again, that's okay.

But with time, you will almost certainly accept the death and still be able to function.

(e) TURN STRESS AROUND

Once you have worked your way through these five grief stages, it is time to ask yourself the bigger questions.

▸ Why has this happened to me?
▸ What have I learnt from this experience?
▸ Is there anything about this experience that I can use to my advantage?

The old saying 'Every cloud has a silver lining' very much pertains to this situation.

I experienced a basic example of this a few years ago, in the days before terrorist attacks on planes.

I was on a flight to Malaysia, where in two days' time I was to deliver a lecture. When I lecture overseas, I always like to arrive the day before my talk in case there are delays or problems at the airports.

I was sitting on the plane at around 10 pm, waiting for take-off. After what seemed an awfully long time, the pilot announced there was a mechanical problem which would prevent the flight leaving.

There I was, grounded at Sydney airport. It was 11 pm by the time I retrieved my luggage. I live on the other side of Sydney harbour, around 45 minutes from the airport. It was Tuesday night and I was lecturing first thing Thursday morning on the Malaysian island of Langkawi – two flights away from Sydney.

Should I go home? Should I stay at an airport hotel overnight? Could I make it in time to Malaysia? Were there any seats available on other flights?

Rather than reacting in anger or becoming upset about something over which I had no control, I decided to go home to my own bed and let my manager deal with the situation first thing in the morning. I rang the Speakers Bureau at 9 am, I was on a plane at 1 pm and arrived at Langkawi late on Wednesday evening.

On the flight from Sydney to Kuala Lumpur, I was reading one of my cardiology journals. The male flight attendant noticed the journal and asked me if I was a cardiologist. He then went on to explain that he was having problems with his blood pressure. I had a long conversation with him, explaining many aspects of hypertension, and he was very grateful.

As we started the descent into Kuala Lumpur, the flight attendant invited me into the cockpit for the landing. It was a spectacular experience – one I would not have had if I had been on the plane the previous night. Incidentally, the flight attendant is now a loyal patient of mine with very well-controlled blood pressure!

This is a fairly straightforward example of being able to turn around an acute stress and make it a positive. I'm not suggesting that every acute stress will always result in such a gratifying conclusion, but I am suggesting that with each stress come important life lessons. If you approach these stresses in the correct fashion, you will inevitably grow from the experience.

2 MAKE THE MOST OF YOUR TIME

One of the major complaints of most people in modern society is lack of time. The reasons for this are obvious. As life becomes more complex, these complex activities take more time. Take the example of parenting in our modern age. When I was a child, I used to ride my bike to school. But with the ever-increasing urban sprawl, children are less likely to live particularly close to school, meaning that they have to catch public transport or be driven there. And as parents who drive their kids to school know, making the daily trip, often during peak-hour traffic, takes a significant amount of time out of the parent's morning.

Children are often involved in activities after school on almost every weekday, not to mention Saturday morning sport. Parents are usually the unpaid taxi drivers for the children, as well as donating their time to perform various voluntary tasks at the children's school.

Parenting is not the only area where more demands are being made on our time. Take the current corporate culture. It's not unusual for those in the corporate world to arrive at work somewhere between 7 and 8 am and not leave the office until well after 7 pm, perhaps even later.

In chapter 2, on energy, I suggested human beings have enough energy stores for around eight hours of active energy, eight hours' relaxation and then need to sleep for around eight hours. Whether you are a full-time parent or engaged in a high-level job in the corporate world – or, for that matter, any form of employment – it is pretty obvious that usually you're spending much more than eight hours of your day engaged in rather active, energy-sapping activities. The big question then comes: how best can you manage your time in a world where our time is being increasingly eroded?

I would suggest you consider the way you manage your time, using the following principles:

(a) time management
(b) daily quiet time
(c) regular breaks
(d) time away
(e) holidays.

(a) TIME MANAGEMENT

Although many people spend twelve or more hours per day during the week at work, often this time is spent inefficiently. Just to give you a few examples, although I believe it is important to have good working relationships with your fellow workers, how much time do you spend discussing your social life, your antagonisms with those in the hierarchy at work, or possibly the hierarchy at home, or other issues that are not particularly relevant to the job at hand?

How much time do you waste at the water cooler, the morning tea break, or for the more health-damaging habits like ducking outside to have a cigarette? Although I feel it is important to develop work relationships, I also believe it is important to strike a reasonable balance.

When I was more consistently on call at the hospital, on the rare occasions I had to make an after-hours visit, I would always see the same consultants performing their rounds, often at 8 or 9 pm. What I found strange, however, was that these consultants were often having social chats with fellow doctors about matters completely unrelated to patient care. I couldn't help but feel that this time would have been better spent at home with their families. How much time do you spend at work involved in these social chats?

As for any problem, the first step is recognition of the problem. After that, make a decision to rid yourself of a behaviour that is not serving you well. Learning to be more efficient in all activities immediately affords you more time to spend on life-sustaining activities.

Spend a day at work assessing your time-management skills. Become aware of how much you're actually engaged in specific work-related activities and how much you are socialising with your co-workers.

Another great time-waster is meetings. Consider this carefully: how much time do you spend in meetings where people are intent on displaying their egos rather than on making constructive comments or suggestions? If you're in a position of authority, ensure whatever meeting you are involved in has useful aims and structure along with defined time limits for contributions from all those involved.

Dr Edward de Bono has suggested the use of his 'six thinking hats' as an excellent method to structure meetings. Using a structured approach will markedly increase the efficiency of meetings and allow you much more time to perform more important work-related activities.

Regardless of the sphere of work you're involved in, plan your time efficiently. Try to share your responsibilities and learn to delegate activities rather than take on the entire workload yourself.

(b) DAILY QUIET TIME

It is my firm opinion that you should discipline yourself to have 30 minutes of quiet time every day. There are numerous activities you can perform during this time but suffice to say they should involve cranking your brain down to minimal activity. I spend 30 minutes each day meditating, but this may not be your preferred technique.

Sitting quietly in a room listening to Mozart, a relaxation tape, or playing a musical instrument can also achieve a similar benefit. Some people obtain a meditative benefit from watering the garden or even sitting on their back porch and taking in the view.

I will discuss in chapter 10 ('Creative solutions') the techniques and benefits of this regular practice of meditative quiet time.

(c) REGULAR BREAKS

No matter what activity you're performing, you need regular breaks throughout the time you are engaged in that activity. These may be as simple as a toilet break, getting up from your desk and stretching for a minute or so, or even going for a short walk. Regular breaks refocus your brain, allowing your concentration and thought

IN WITH THE GOOD

processes to be more efficient. Try taking a short break of a few minutes after each half-hour of sustained activity. I promise you, your work will be much more rewarding and efficient using this system.

(d) TIME AWAY

People these days often work six and at times even seven days a week. Having a weekend – or if you can manage it, a long weekend – away every couple of months is vital to recharge the batteries. During that time you should discipline yourself to dislocate yourself from work. Don't leave contact numbers with anyone other than your family and friends. It is my regular practice to have either one or two nights away with my wife, without the children, every few months. Often on other occasions we will take the children away for a few days.

If you can afford it, a night in an international hotel in the city is a wonderful escape. Many people do not enjoy the benefits of their own city. Experience what the tourists are raving about!

(e) HOLIDAYS

I was holidaying on the New South Wales north coast. As I was walking past one of the villas at the resort in which I was staying, I saw and overheard a man on a mobile telephone saying, 'I have a fax machine in my room and if you want to fax the documents through I will analyse them and send you a report.' It was two days before Christmas and I realised that this man, although allegedly on holidays, was still working.

Although what he was doing was no doubt urgent, I equally have no doubt that the whole scenario was not serving him particularly well. When you go on holidays, my advice is very simple: have a holiday. By definition, a holiday is a break from your normal activities.

A number of years ago I was holidaying on the Gold Coast of Queensland. I made the mistake of taking my mobile phone purely to order pizza. Instead I was receiving around five calls per day from the hospital. I also received a phone call from Bangkok, from a patient wanting to discuss whether he should or shouldn't have bypass surgery. I spent twenty minutes on the phone, at my expense, as I returned his call and tried to convince this man that he needed the operation.

After these incidents, I promised myself I would not take my mobile on holidays again. What I'm saying here is obvious – it doesn't matter what your life occupation or position, we all need time away for more than a day or two from our normal day-to-day activities. I will see the occasional patient who proudly says to me, 'Doctor, I haven't had a holiday in ten years.' My reply to this statement is, 'Well, you're an idiot!'

No, I don't really say this, but it's certainly what I'm thinking. When you decide to have a holiday, make sure you spend a considerable amount of this time in pure relaxation.

3 DECLUTTER YOUR LIFE

A simple principle in life is to make life as simple as possible. I believe it is vital to declutter your life. A messy life is a major cause of stress. So many people live in cluttered homes. A cluttered house is an indication of a cluttered life. Too often, we overload ourselves with activities and responsibilities and spend most of the day dealing with the more urgent matters arising from these varied activities.

One of the most important words you need to learn in this regard is 'no'. If being involved in a particular activity is of no real benefit to you, then say, 'As much as I would like to help, I'm far too busy to really contribute my energy to this project.'

If your study is full of unread journals, throw them out. You will almost certainly never read them and every time you walk into your study they are just a reminder of your inability to manage your time efficiently.

A good principle in this regard is if you have not used a piece of equipment, read a specific journal, or been involved in a particular activity, for twelve months or more then give away, sell or throw out the material involved. If later you find that you want the material (and you probably won't), you can always purchase a brand new, upgraded version.

4 BE POSITIVE AND MAINTAIN A SENSE OF HUMOUR

As I said in the previous chapter, negativity breeds negativity. Conversely, positivity breeds positivity. The more you can engender positive attitudes in yourself and those around you, the more you will view occurrences in your life as positive. If you see setbacks as opportunities to try a different approach, I can assure you, you will notice fewer setbacks as time goes on.

Most of us enjoy a good laugh. Good-natured humour is a vital part of improving your stress management techniques. Telling jokes, listening to a funny comedian or watching a comedy on television or at the movies are all great ways to release the endorphins.

5 CREATE BALANCE THROUGH SELF-DEVELOPMENT AND SELF-CARE

I believe a very powerful way to achieve balance in your life is to get involved in activities outside home and work. These include hobbies, sport, music, art and exploring all the wonderful aspects of nature. Despite being in my late forties, I still play soccer and am very passionate about the game. I love Saturday afternoons during winter when I kick a ball around with my mates in the local competition. Although some of my colleagues treat their game like it's the World Cup, for me it is pure pleasure; my time away from work and from home.

Giving yourself this time to pursue an interest is an important aspect of self-care. The nature of the activity is less important than the fact that you are setting aside time to pursue – and enjoy – that activity.

The Walker rule number one of medicine is very straightforward: 'The most important coronary arteries in this world are your own.'

If you don't look after yourself, no-one else is going to bother. How much of your time do you spend concerning yourself with work matters or home matters and in reality how much of your time do you spend in activities that will sustain your life?

How much attention do you give to your nutrition? How much time do you spend each week exercising? How much time do you spend practising stress management techniques? If the answer to these questions is 'not much' – and I suspect in most cases it is – I would strongly suggest you re-evaluate your priorities.

My previous book, *The Cell Factor*, clearly offers you a sensible life plan for achieving optimum physical health. *The Life Factor* offers you the plan to achieve the same results in all aspects of your life. I see every day as an opportunity for self-development, and I believe that after following the suggestions offered in this book, so will you.

ACTION SUMMARY

Don't just lose the bad – replace it with the good. See acute stress as an opportunity for the progression of your character.

Take time out! Don't just wait for that holiday at the end of the year; make sure you carefully plan each day so that you have time for activities that enrich you.

Simplify your life by getting rid of the clutter that is of no value to you anyway.

As the Monty Python team said in *The Life of Brian*, always look on the bright side of life.

And finally, see each day as an opportunity for personal growth. Nurture your most valuable asset – you!

CHAPTER 9

Which planet are you from?

Relationships occur at many levels. In many ways, our life is an ongoing relationship. In this chapter, I discuss the importance of relationships in shaping our lifelong reaction to stress. I will consider relationships at five levels:

1 primary partner
2 family and close friends
3 others
4 self
5 higher being.

1 PRIMARY PARTNER

Attendant with society's increasing complexities and stresses is the fact of ever-increasing relationship breakdown. In fact, there are not many people these days who can claim a lifelong partnership with another person.

Unfortunately, we are not supplied with a user manual for our relationships. Mind you, even when a user manual is supplied for some gadgets, many of us still have problems!

2 FAMILY AND CLOSE FRIENDS

It is my strong opinion that each of us is born with an individual personality and character traits. I do, however, believe that the excesses and deficits of our behaviour are mainly determined by our experiences in the early years of our life.

The proverb says, 'Give me a child for seven years and you may do what you like with him afterwards.' I totally agree with this proverb – give or take a few years.

Obviously, our experiences over our early years are many and varied, but it is during this time that we develop the basic behavioural building blocks that will determine our reactions to whatever life will present.

As we have seen in chapter 4, our parents (or our primary male and female role models) are vital in shaping these reactions. The skill of being a good parent or role model is to recognise the strengths and weaknesses of the child, accentuate the strengths and minimise the weaknesses.

Returning to the 'user manual' concept, there is no specific user manual to instruct adults on how to be good parents and role models. Nobody is perfect; I have certainly never spoken to anybody who can claim to have had a perfect childhood.

For the greater part, your deepest emotions are reserved for your primary partner, other family members and your close friends. These friends are an integral part of the deep emotional bonds which help sustain the emotional balance that is so necessary for a fulfilling life.

Close friends are those people who always seem to be there when you need them. Just like close family members, they share your joys and successes but also your pain during times of trouble.

It is my strong advice to always nurture these friendships. I believe the essence of true friendship can be summed up in one word: giving. Always be prepared to put yourself out for your friends. Your true friends will always be prepared to do the same for you.

3 OTHERS

Many hours of the day are often spent interacting with people who do not fit any of the above criteria, such as work colleagues, casual acquaintances or the numerous people you deal with in shops, on the streets, or on the telephone.

You may see these people as insignificant in the grand scheme of your existence but in my opinion each interaction, major or minor, is a learning experience.

Approach each person with courtesy and respect and you will soon realise the difference in your life. Start every interaction with the reasonable premise that no-one is insignificant and your view of life will change. A kind word, a thoughtful gesture at the right time, may be the difference between someone else having a profoundly positive or negative experience.

My beautiful daughter, Alexandra, has a wonderful spirit that shows itself in so many ways. A man in his sixties, whom she barely knows, was chatting with her at work the other day. He informed her that he was having coronary bypass surgery the following Monday. He then went on to tell Alexandra that his wife had died a few years before and both his sons live too far away to help him through the operation and during the recovery.

Alexandra then offered to pick him up from hospital on discharge and drive him home. Her profound generosity deeply touched this man. Show people you care.

See every interaction, no matter how small, as a test of your character. A positive contribution to the wellbeing of others – even people you don't really know – can have profound benefits, not only for them but also for the course of your own life, I promise you.

4 SELF

Throughout your entire life the only person you will never be able to avoid is yourself. Try to see every day as a self-improvement program. Learn to respect yourself in every sense. If you owned a million-dollar racehorse, would you feed it bad food, cigarettes, keep it up all night drinking and stress it beyond belief? Of course you wouldn't – it would be a total waste of such a valuable asset.

Unfortunately, many people do not have the respect and discipline to treat themselves in the same fashion as they would treat their prize racehorse, or any other valuable asset.

Monitor the internal and external language you use to describe yourself. How many times do you describe yourself as a 'fool' or an 'idiot'? How often do you deride yourself for not achieving your goals? Start to turn this around immediately.

Remember, unless you can respect and contribute to your own existence and wellbeing, you cannot make any reasonable contributions to the greater good.

5 HIGHER BEING

This is the most straightforward relationship we could possibly develop. Either there is a God or there is no God. There is no absolute proof either way, so it is purely an individual decision which side of the belief fence you decide to sit on.

The atheistic sceptics argue strongly that the sole purpose of belief in a higher being is to make the believers more comfortable with their fear of death. They see religion as a sophisticated form of crowd control.

It is not my position to push any religious barrow but I am happy to state that I do believe in God and I know this belief gives my existence a purpose. Having a belief in a force greater than yourself gives your life a different perspective. It helps you to realise that as living beings, we are all connected through this higher force.

People often blame religion for much of the world's ills. Many of the wars and conflicts throughout history have been fuelled by religious differences. Although this is historical fact – and is still the case, as anyone who watches television knows – it is not God's fault. The bigotry and hatred arising from differing religious doctrines is a man-made, ego-based creation and has little to do (some would say nothing to do) with our true personal relationship with God.

FOCUS ON YOUR PRIMARY PARTNER

What is it that attracts us to our primary life partner? People offer many reasons but I believe that the workings of attraction are far too intangible to be explained. Whatever the rational reason, there is something about our primary partner that separates them from all other human beings with whom we interact.

During the honeymoon phase of your relationship, the passion is running high. It is difficult to concentrate on anything else because most of your emotional energy is directed towards your partner. It is a reality of human physiology that this emotional high cannot be sustained. If a deeper love evolves over time, the emotions are still there but obviously not to the same extreme as experienced at the beginning of the relationship.

So, if you can feel such a rush at the start of your primary relationship, and this settles to a deeper, ongoing love, why do so many relationships crumble, often to the point of bitter hatred?

One answer is: the higher the peak, the lower the trough. Although there is probably some truth in that statement, I believe it is far too simplistic. Modern society brings its own set of problems but we must be realistic. Human beings since recorded history have not been particularly flash at maintaining peaceful, loving, harmonious relationships on many levels. Getting this part right is one of the most difficult aspects of life.

Let's consider the reasons relationships go bad:

1 responsibility
2 routine
3 life crises
4 personal baggage
5 ongoing problems.

1 RESPONSIBILITY

Many of us choose to wander through life with a partner. The size, shape, form and sex of that partner is entirely a matter of your and their choosing, and nobody else's business.

The old saying 'Beauty is in the eye of the beholder' certainly allows us a broad canvas in the choice of a partner. But, once you have made the decision that Bill, Jean, Clara, George or whoever is the one with whom you would like to share your life experiences, one thing is absolutely certain. No long-term relationship will move along without any hitches.

Once a relationship starts, so does the other big 'R' word – responsibility. No longer are you responsible solely for your own life and your own actions, you are now either directly or indirectly responsible for the actions of your partner. The most common long-term relationships are between members of the opposite sex and therefore there is a good chance that these long-term relationships will also include children. With the increasing rates of separation and divorce, often there are children from previous relationships. So, when you make the big decision to commit to a relationship, you might also take on responsibility for a pre-prepared family (as if the responsibility for just one other person wasn't enough).

Let's face it – responsibility sucks!

When you first start on that magical road called love, the major responsibilities consist of maintaining the passion, finding the time to be together at the expense of your usual life and starting to understand the person with whom you fully intend to devote a considerable amount of your time and energy.

Once you make a commitment to each other for a long-term relationship, then the responsibilities begin: shared finances, living together, spending, saving, new acquisitions, holidays. After making firm commitments, the biggest conjoint responsibility occurs – the decision to marry and/or have children, or to accept responsibility for the children your partner already has.

Ongoing disagreements and fights over money and children often lead to increasing tension between partners. The strain on a relationship created by financial difficulties or difficult children can do irreparable damage.

CASE STUDY – TRENT AND DIANE

Trent and Diane met at university. Both were excellent students who performed well in their respective courses. Their love grew over many months and they soon became an item at numerous social events within and outside the campus. After completion of their courses, they both commenced work. Their relationship suffered the typical ups and downs of most couples but they were extremely devoted to each other and after six years together, they decided to marry.

By their late twenties, their combined income saw them in a comfortable position, able to afford their first mortgage and contemplate their first child. Within a few months, Diane was pregnant and excited about motherhood. Although also delighted, Trent hid his concern regarding the financial burden of a mortgage, the responsibilities of a child and the loss of Diane's income when the baby was born, as they had already decided Diane would stop working until their child was old enough to attend school.

After the birth of the baby, reality set in. Diane was constantly tired, as the baby was an erratic sleeper. Before they had been very comfortable; now they struggled to afford the lifestyle to which they were accustomed. Trent's sports car was replaced with a station wagon with room for the baby capsule. Their lovemaking became non-existent due to Diane's fatigue and her recovery from some gynaecological problems as a result of a difficult childbirth.

The fights began and despite their many good years together, Trent and Diane were on the verge of separation. It was quite a turn-around from the model couple seen during their earlier, more care-free days. The responsibility of children and their attendant complications had taken its toll on their relationship.

2 ROUTINE

One of the great killers of passion is routine. The human brain is wired for novelty. If I played you a beautiful song, at the first few listenings you would feel that rush, that wonderful tingling of enjoyment.

Unfortunately, after you have heard the song on numerous occasions, it does not have the same effect. In the same way, a great meal stimulates the taste buds, but if you eat it every night, it loses some of its piquancy. Get over it – it's physiology! This physiology, however, is a major cause for relationship breakdown.

The thrill of a new relationship as opposed to the sameness and routine of a long-term relationship cannot be denied. The reality is, however, that novelty will always be replaced by familiarity. Constantly chasing the short-term high of a new relationship usually results in long-term pain for those who never come to realise that passion can be superseded by a deeper and more abiding love.

The brain wiring that provides the short-term rush is the identical pleasure–reward–motivation system that I discussed in chapter 1 and in the section on addiction in chapter 7. Acute passion, whether condoned in an established relationship or frowned upon in an illicit relationship, is in many ways the satisfaction of the addictive response.

The real skill is allowing this addictive response to work for you within your established relationship and not to look for it outside that relationship. Affairs, mistresses, prostitutes and casual one-night stands have been rife in many societies since recorded history began but I believe this is yet another example of the primitive nature of our emotional responses.

CASE STUDY – TRENT AND DIANE CONTINUED

After the initial resolution of Trent and Diane's marital disharmony (mainly through time and a few brief visits to a marriage counsellor), Diane fell pregnant again. During this pregnancy, Diane gained a considerable amount of weight, developed gestational diabetes and required a Caesarean section for the birth. In the post-partum period, she developed a moderate depression that saw Trent trying to juggle his increasingly responsible job with his difficult home life.

His previously attractive wife was now depressed and overweight. There was no sex life and two demanding children. Their relationship was in tatters. Trent felt his life was on a treadmill. He dreaded going home to screaming children and a depressed wife.

Diane, on the other hand, was near suicide. She felt no real support from Trent who, although he was a good father, showed no understanding or compassion for her feelings. He had no comprehension of the profound effects of depression.

Trent, in his early thirties, maintained a healthy body and striking good looks. Kate started working in his office as a receptionist. She had stunning looks and long blonde hair, with a body to die for. Kate had enjoyed male attention for as long as she could remember and soon the histrionics between her and Trent began.

It wasn't long before the blatant flirting became drinks after work. Trent then began increasingly to 'work back'. You can guess the rest.

This very common scenario is a major cause of relationship breakdown. The routine (some would say drudgery) of everyday life, combined with the responsibilities which go hand in hand with this routine, often drive people to seek an escape and a return to the old passionate rush experienced when they were younger.

3 LIFE CRISES

Most analyses of life crises rank the top three as follows:

- death of a loved one
- infidelity
- major life change such as changing jobs, moving house/cities, divorce or separation.

Any major crisis in your life creates enormous strain on relationships. Many relationships break down as a consequence of such crises. I believe, though, that we can work through life crises using the techniques outlined in this book. It is possible to not only come through crisis but to experience personal growth and ultimately benefit from the experience.

4 PERSONAL BAGGAGE

A reality of any relationship is the fact that it involves the contributions of two individuals. Each individual brings into the relationship their own personal baggage. This baggage includes all of the following:

(a) specific personality/character traits
(b) preceding life situation
(c) specific life traumas
(d) personal expectations of love
(e) role models.

Each of these factors contributes to the manner in which each individual will behave within a relationship. Let's look briefly at examples from each category.

(a) One partner will crave affection and will love to be the centre of attention, whilst the other, though highly devoted, prefers to demonstrate their affection through less visible acts of loyalty and devotion.

(b) A busy, demanding career may mean less focus by one partner on the relationship.

(c) An abused child often becomes a psychologically abused or abusive adult.

(d) For one partner, love may mean intense possessiveness and a sense of ownership, whereas the other partner brings to the relationship the concept of love as allowing the other person a distinct sense of freedom.

(e) Your major role models throughout your childhood usually subliminally instil in you a distinct sense of how males and females should behave within a relationship. I'm not suggesting men select women like their mothers and women select men like their fathers, but there are strong influences either towards or away from the examples set by these role models.

5 ONGOING PROBLEMS

Particular problems are often taken into relationships. These problems may not emerge until the stress and responsibilities begin. For example, problems such as excessive alcohol intake, drug addiction or problem gambling are extremely disruptive to any relationship. The co-dependency created by such problems accentuates the pathological nature of these relationships.

Unless these conditions can be controlled, there is usually distinct relationship breakdown.

THE BENEFITS OF A PRIMARY RELATIONSHIP

So, with all the potential pitfalls, you may ask, why would anyone want to be involved at this level with another human being? Well, the obvious answer is, there are enormous benefits. If nurtured properly, a primary relationship can sustain you for the rest of your life. I believe having a strong primary relationship with another person offers you the following five benefits:

1 deep friendship
2 shared responsibility
3 procreation
4 physical satisfaction
5 fulfilment.

1 DEEP FRIENDSHIP

If you have the privilege of a truly functional relationship, you'll understand the joy of spending time with your partner. Sharing the highs and lows of your life with this person can heighten the joy and lessen the pain.

Travelling through life's journey without this friendship may make for a very lonely existence.

When you have been hurt by something in your life, the first thought that comes to mind is unburdening yourself by telling your partner. You know they care as much about *you* as you do. Equally, when you have achieved a personal triumph, you know your partner will be just as excited.

Discussing and trusting your most intimate thoughts and feelings with your partner is always an enriching experience and an opportunity for personal growth. I believe this is one of the great values of a long-term, intense relationship. The shared history, respect and caring that come from years of bonding are very special and need constant nurturing.

2 SHARED RESPONSIBILITY

Responsibility, as we have seen, is often one of the major downsides, sometimes even the death knell, of an initially sound relationship. Sharing responsibilities can lessen the trauma of these burdens.

In our modern world, many families require two incomes in order to afford and maintain a good quality of life. Unfortunately, due to old-style thinking, many of the responsibilities for maintenance of the home fall back on women.

If both partners are working, surely there should be an equitable division of labour when it comes to domestic duties. Sharing these responsibilities makes life easier for both parties, and certainly strengthens the relationship.

3 PROCREATION

One of the greatest blessings in life is having children and then watching them grow into functional, happy adults. I believe strongly that the best start you can give your children is to have a strong, happy parental relationship.

Sharing your children's pain and triumphs, together, is a profound, rewarding experience. Unfortunately, however, we're living in a society where divorce and separation are rife. My plea to the many people who suffer these traumas is to try your hardest to minimise the effects on your children.

Any bitterness you may feel toward your partner under these circumstances should not be transferred to your children. Don't use them as pawns in a destructive game, because these situations can scar children for life.

4 PHYSICAL SATISFACTION

A functional relationship is almost always the setting for ongoing affection and mutual sexual satisfaction. Maintain the passion in your relationship by ensuring you have time alone as a couple. In your busy life, you can become so caught up with work and children that your primary relationship suffers. You no longer plan romantic dinners together or have weekends away without the children, and your lovemaking becomes an occasional afterthought when both of you are too tired to enjoy it.

In many ways, you need to designate time for yourselves because, if you don't, you'll find that the reason it all started in the first place – your relationship – is no longer.

5 FULFILMENT

The first four points each contribute strongly to the final point here: a healthy primary relationship delivers deep, inner fulfilment. As I have stated constantly throughout this book, we are all striving to achieve a major purpose in life, to feel the inner peace and contentment that I call the Life Factor.

Although I do not believe we should expect other people to create purpose for us, being involved in an ongoing deep, personal relationship with another person contributes markedly to finding and maintaining this state.

So, how do we achieve quality in our relationships? Here is the Five-Step Action Plan:

1 **Accept differences.**
2 **Improve your communication skills.**
3 **Forgive.**
4 **Let your partner become your best friend.**
5 **Value the other person's position.**

1 ACCEPT DIFFERENCES

The world-famous author John Gray has built his career around the lateral thinking suggestion that 'women are from Venus and men are from Mars' – a concept that obviously suggests our differences are extreme. Although this concept is useful to some extent, I would like to proffer the suggestion that because each *individual* is so different, we should extend the planetary metaphor somewhat. We would need an entire universe of planets, stars and the occasional renegade asteroid to describe the diversity of human behaviour.

People do the strangest things, especially when it comes to relationships. I'm not just talking about adult male–female relationships but all manner of relationships, including our first with dear old mum, to casual friendships, right up to the big decision, let's spend the rest of our days together types.

Relationships come in all permutations and with varying levels of importance. Volumes have been written on the importance of relationships at all levels and I'm certainly not going to try to re-invent the wheel or summarise the major works in the area. This book is about stress – and relationships can be one of the major sources of stress in our lives.

As I have already stated in chapter 4, it is our relationship with our parents, especially our mother, which shapes our reaction to all future relationships. Unfortunately we don't have a huge amount of control over this particular number. It is thought by some that we 'pick' our parents before birth. If that is the case, some of us made a very hurried decision.

There is no doubting the truth of the old adage, 'We are all victims of victims', but the buck must stop with us.

One of the major tests of life is to overcome the excesses and deficits of our upbringing. Some people are able to overcome this whilst others fail, plunging themselves into addiction, neuroses, crime, or character disorders.

Terry is 24. He is the younger brother in a family of two boys. His older brother is 27 and from an early age showed talent in many areas. Unfortunately the boys' father was an alcoholic who frequently physically abused their mother – and when he was finished with her, he would often turn on the boys. Terry seemed to be more of a target than his elder brother and would often attend his primary school bruised from the previous night's beating. As he progressed through his schooling, he became the school bully and in his mid-teens the main drug dealer; all the while his older brother was excelling academically. For those unaware of his home situation, there was amazement at the difference between the brothers.

Terry was expelled in Year 10 following a nasty beating that he dished out to a year 9 boy who would not pay some money he owed. Within a couple of years, Terry's continued antisocial and illegal activities had resulted in a jail term.

After his release from jail, Terry drifted from mundane job to job, experiencing the typical frustration that an intelligent non-achiever would feel under the circumstances.

Terry derived a sense of hopelessness from his childhood, but his older brother perceived the need to perform in order to overcome the traumas of his early life. I'm not suggesting Terry's brother was a saint, but his problems were less overt than Terry's and his coping mechanisms were better. What I am suggesting is that the problems of Terry and his brother were a direct result of their early life situation; the difference between the two was how they coped with the early suffering.

THE MALE AND FEMALE BRAIN

There is no doubt that the male and female brains are wired differently. The best summary of this major discrepancy is that women tend to think globally and men tend to think in compartments. When a man is on the job, that's exactly where he is. Don't ask him to do anything else at the time, by the way, because it won't happen.

Have you ever tried to disturb a male whilst he's watching television? His hand is firmly grasped around the remote control and he's in the television viewing zone. Any attempt at conversation during this particular mode is completely ignored by the male and should be avoided by the female. He can probably manage a guttural noise or grunt, but don't expect any registration at the cerebral level or any recollection of the conversation at a later stage. The connection with the remote control, however, is a much more pressing issue. This is known medically as the oculo-digital reflex and allows minimal exposure to seemingly useless pieces of advertising known as commercials that may inadvertently disrupt the focus on whatever particular sporting event is the subject of the television coverage. The male may stumble on re-runs of *Baywatch* during the commercials, which, of course, makes the exercise worthwhile.

Yes, the above example is facetious, but it also illustrates an important point. Although to the majority of the female species this characteristic male behaviour does not appear to serve much purpose, it is actually useful in many situations.

The ability to focus one's complete attention on a single activity allows precise attention to detail, determination and persistence. Thus, many great achievements throughout history can be attributed to this ability. Although I'm not suggesting a similar resolve does not occur in women, it is often not as strong a characteristic. (Please, don't start writing nasty letters or sending abusive emails. There also have been, of course, many great female achievers throughout the ages.)

So, the big question is: is there any biological, evolutionary reason why the male brain is wired differently to the female brain? The answer is yes.

Let me first state that most of what I am about to argue is a generalisation; there are always exceptions. During prehistoric times when men and women were hunter–gatherers, the name of the game was survival. Whether the male evolved with a greater muscle mass or whether generations of being the main food gatherer led to a greater muscle mass, the reality was that he was the stronger, more physically capable member of the species.

If you give testosterone (the main male hormone) to a female, she develops much larger muscles, more body hair and a deep voice. She becomes stronger. (Please do not try this at home!) In the same way, if you take away a man's testosterone supply or give him female hormones, he loses his muscle mass, develops breasts, loses body hair and develops a high voice.

One defining characteristic for males is their inability to conceive children. The reason for this is blatantly obvious – males don't have the correct childbearing apparatus. Again, you guessed it – it's all about biology.

Thus, the taller, stronger, smarter males make the best hunters, and back in the very old days were probably considered the best catches by the females of the species – not only because they were the best providers, but also because they offered the best chance to pass on these characteristics to their offspring.

Again – take a bow, Charles Darwin – it's all about the survival of the species through survival of the fittest.

Females have evolved biologically to be nurturers. This global, intuitive style of thinking and feeling instils a much keener sense of caring for her vulnerable, small children. One of the first acts of motherhood is for the mother to share her internal environment with a growing child. The newly conceived life form implants itself in the lining of her uterus and she supplies its needs in terms of oxygen and nourishment at her own expense. Sharing is, therefore, an inherent behaviour of the female. I am in no way suggesting men don't share, but they are not as biologically primed to do so.

Thus, the distinct characteristics of a woman stem from this innate ability to share and nurture. Ever since women started producing babies, they not only required a keen sense of their own environment but also the same, finely honed sense of the child's environment. How many women do you know who can talk on the phone whilst they cook dinner, attend to a crying child and drink a cup of tea? People pay buskers to see that kind of thing and call it talent. I call it being a woman. It's innate stuff.

Men are therefore concrete, focused, uni-dimensional beasts with an enormous capacity for logical thought. Women, on the other hand, are global, empathetic, caring, multi-dimensional beasts with, at times, the demonstration of somewhat fuzzy logic. It's biology – get over it and accept it!

There are so many variations on the gross theme of the differences between men and women, but, in reality, it all comes down to a few very basic concepts. We've already talked about gender and upbringing; personality is another major player.

Anyone who comes from a large family or has a number of children will understand clearly that each member of a family has a distinct personality despite being reared by the same parents and under similar environmental circumstances.

Whatever the reason for these distinct personalities, they do exist and need to be recognised. You cannot travel through life expecting everyone you interact with to think and feel the same way as yourself. One of the major problems with modern society is the inability to respect these differences, both at a global and personal level.

2 IMPROVE YOUR COMMUNICATION SKILLS

No doubt you've heard thousands of times about the importance of communication. But, guess what, the greatest problem in any relationship is poor communication. So although volumes have been written and spoken about this issue, it still seems that we humans aren't particularly good at communicating.

So many people either lose their cool over seemingly trivial issues or, at the other extreme, bottle up their feelings, denying the other party in the relationship any insight into the situation.

Sometimes it can be quite painful and traumatic to disclose your opinion, especially if it may be hurtful or bruise the ego of the recipient, but, in many ways, the acute trauma that is sometimes the result of frank communication is preferable to prolonged lack of communication and thus continual erosion of what may otherwise be a very good relationship.

3 FORGIVE

Because we live in an imperfect world, there is always the strong potential for mistakes to be made. Many mistakes are trivial and easily corrected. Some, however, justify inclusion into the 'mistake hall of fame'. If you're the recipient of this kind of mistake, the most healing act you can perform for yourself is to forgive.

As I mentioned in chapter 3, one of the major thrusts of the work of the medical intuitive, Caroline Myss, is that of 'woundology'. Myss talks about people who, for whatever reason, were traumatised as children and then carry that trauma for many years. Their major raison d'être is to live out this trauma. They join abuse support groups, fight for victims' rights and basically wear their wound on their sleeve rather than moving on with their life.

No-one is condoning or supporting any form of abuse, but to forgive and move on is incredibly healing, not only for the perpetrator of the crime, but more so for the victim. Once the victim has forgiven, they can begin a new life beyond the effects of the abuse.

4 LET YOUR PARTNER BECOME YOUR BEST FRIEND

If your best mate came to you and said, 'I hate my job, it drives me crazy, the people I work with are intolerable and I find it deathly boring,' you would probably say, 'You've got to leave – take the risk, find a new job.'

If your partner came to you with the same complaint, you would immediately think twice about the mortgage, the bills, school fees and so on.

I'm not suggesting you throw caution to the wind and allow your partner total freedom to pursue any avenue of life they may desire, but I also believe it is important not to be stifled by a career or situation that prevents any opportunity for personal growth. Seeing your partner as your best friend allows you to approach these issues from this perspective.

5 VALUE THE OTHER PERSON'S POSITION

It is unusual for both parties within a relationship to have equal financial earning status, equal job status or even equal societal status.

This is especially so when you consider the traditional family structure with one partner, usually (but not always) the male, working and the other partner staying at home to pursue domestic duties.

In many ways, this latter role is devalued by society and subconsciously devalued by the money-earning partner. One of my good friends, who is also one of Australia's financial gurus, has been trying for years to convince the insurance industry to introduce some type of disability insurance to cover mothers who become ill. Unfortunately, no-one in the industry is particularly interested.

The 'domestic supervisor' who in reality keeps the family together deserves more credit for the invaluable service she (and at times, he) performs. The money-earning partner could not perform his or her tasks without this unpaid support. I believe it is vital to respect and value this work.

My wife has devoted most of her adult life to being the mother of our children. It is my firm belief that her devotion to this calling is the main reason we have five wonderful, well-adjusted children. I value what she has done and continues to do, and I think that in many ways, my appreciation and respect contribute to her energy and enthusiasm towards this vital part of our lives.

We should value and affirm the worth of all the other people with whom we share relationships.

ACTION SUMMARY

Are you happy with your current relationships – with your partner, your family, friends and acquaintances and with yourself and your concept of God? If not, think very carefully about the points outlined in this chapter. In your Life Journal, write down the main issues, as you see them, and start to formulate some solutions.

When thinking about the issues, you may want to apply the Five-Step Action Plan for ridding yourself of bad coping mechanisms, detailed in chapter 7. *Decide* what you want from your relationships; *interrupt* the limiting patterns; *create* a new pattern; *condition* the pattern until you have a normal, functional basis for your relationship; and finally, *live* the program.

CHAPTER 10

Think outside the square: Creative solutions

Through the ages, the greatest minds have challenged conventional thinking. It is the same in the present day – without a creative, new approach to current dilemmas, nothing will change. In this chapter, I will outline some of the many creative ways in which we can approach our problems and formulate solutions.

We can take action in five areas:

1 Learn how to focus.
2 Lead a principle-centred life.
3 Nurture your attitude.
4 Question the thinking–feeling connection.
5 Aim for balance.

1 LEARN HOW TO FOCUS

When we allow the experiences of the past to determine our present lives, we become prisoners to these experiences.

Childhood trauma of any kind can determine many of your current reactions and behaviours, not to mention ongoing psychological trauma which might persist to the present moment.

The spiritual teacher Eckhart Tolle wrote a book called *The Power of Now*, in which he stresses the importance of living in the moment. This is the discipline of being fully present. Focus on your current experience, be aware of your feelings and thoughts as if you were the observer and not just the doer.

Just the simple act of shifting your focus to this position enhances your enjoyment of the moment. Once a fortnight, I indulge myself by having a remedial massage. During the massage, although I am very relaxed, I discipline myself to focus on the area where the masseuse is working. This greatly enhances my enjoyment of the massage.

In the case of negative experiences, becoming the observer can often minimise deleterious effects and make the trauma more neutral. If you are in pain, become the observer; watch the pain. People have been known to minimise the pain of dental or minor surgery by combining this technique with various forms of self-hypnosis. (Mind you, I'd prefer the anaesthetic!)

The art of focus is gradually becoming lost in our modern society. This lost art has become manifest in many of the conditions of modern life.

ATTENTION DEFICIT DISORDER

There is now an epidemic in childhood of a condition termed ADD – attention deficit disorder. It is my opinion (a view not really shared by many experts in the field) that ADD is due to a combination of three factors:

Nutrition: The brain depends on a regular supply of high-quality nutrients for it to function normally. Good-quality fat is essential for high-quality thinking and behaviour.

There is a structure known as the blood–brain barrier which is a fatty layer between – strangely enough – the bloodstream and the brain tissue. Unfortunately, with modern diets we are bombarding the blood–brain barrier with excessive doses of synthetic fats and processed carbohydrates. These synthetic foods, found ubiquitously in our modern processed, packaged diets, thicken and harden the blood–brain barrier and also the membranes covering the nerve cells.

This constant bombardment alters thinking and behaviour, especially in growing brains. Just remember any occasion your child has ingested excessive amounts of junk food after a visit to the local takeaway or a birthday party. The child is wired for a few hours afterwards and often finds it hard to sleep that night.

Many children and teenagers are ingesting somewhere between 10 to 20 per cent of their daily diet in processed sugars and up to 30 per cent in synthetic fats. I believe this is a recipe for all types of behavioural disorders.

Discipline: No-one could or should ever condone violence but in our increasingly unsafe, violent world we have moved to the other extreme regarding the disciplining of children. Parents who raise their voice or don't cater to their child's every whim are seen as akin to child abusers.

A moderate, non-injuring smack across the legs is seen as almost an indictable offence rather than a reasonable method to teach younger children that there are limits. Non-disciplined children invariably lead to non-disciplined adults.

Although I am not advocating constant physical discipline for children, I believe the lack of this form of punishment as a deterrent is part of the reason we are seeing the epidemic of ADD in Western society. There is still a place for the 'spare the rod and spoil the child' approach – as a last resort, and purely used to teach children what is right and what is wrong. If there is no downside to bad behaviour, children will never learn.

Teaching adults to be more effective parents is obviously the best approach but allowing children to 'run riot' is counter-productive for all parties involved.

Lack of focus: One thing you can say for sure about modern society is that none of us is suffering from lack of stimulation. In our world of rapid response and instant gratification, we are bombarded from all angles.

Children these days are overstimulated. If it's not TV or DVDs, it's the numerous facilities available on their computers, from games, to the internet to MSN. Unless there are colours and moving pictures, not to mention the constant thumping of that modern rubbish loosely described as music, children are not satisfied.

The meditative focus of reading, playing a musical instrument, using your own imagination and allowing your senses to be stimulated is vital for normal brain development.

Children are not taught how to focus – instead they are asked to focus on too many things at once. I believe we seriously need to re-evaluate the way we are bringing up our children. I believe we need to restrict television viewing (especially use of the remote control, so they can't watch three to four programs at once!) and aimless computer time and encourage them to spend more time in a meditative focus such as reading. Thank God for Harry Potter!

How has modern society and medicine reacted to ADD? We have taken the easy way out. Instead of recognising it as a side effect of modern life, it is called a disease. The medication that is given to treat ADD is an amphetamine, a form of speed. It works in reverse in children and almost sedates them. So yes, it is an effective Band-aid on a problem but it does not solve the underlying issue. What will happen in a few years' time when these children reach adulthood? Will the medication still be effective? What will happen when the children on ADD medication experiment with alcohol and other drugs? Does anyone really know the long-term safety profile of ADD medications when given to young children? I think not!

Focus is a vital part of your stress management program. Practise, on a daily basis, living in the present moment.

We never really seem to get off the merry-go-round of our existence. Each day we rush from here to there, never really having the
time to finish anything properly. Time has become such an issue
and it is now such an important commodity. Boredom and monot-
ony were once major issues but now in our world we have so many
choices for work, entertainment, leisure, cars – even selecting a cup
of coffee can be an arduous task. You might recall that wonderful
scene from the movie *LA Story* where Steve Martin and his friends
are ordering coffee in every conceivable style, right through to
double decaf with a twist of lemon. Modern-day choices and decisions never stop.

But this constant battle with and against time brings many
important questions, the most important probably being, why do we
exist at all? Do we exist to fill our lives with constant stress and
overload our brains with endless choices – and at the end of the day
still feel exhausted and not really satisfied? Or do we have a deeper
purpose, a more profound reason for existence?

Although I strongly believe we do, I must stress this is purely my
opinion and may be a 'load of cobblers'. But what I do know for
certain is that we will never even scrape the surface of that higher
purpose living in the day-to-day rat-race in which we find ourselves.

The first step to knowing our higher purpose is taking time off
the merry-go-round every day. Just recall what happens when you
take a two-week holiday. The first few days are spent purely winding
down from work. By the end of the second week, however, you're
starting to really feel different. You start to make resolutions like,
I'm not going to work so hard any more, I'm going to read more
novels, I'm going to start painting, I'm going to learn that musical
instrument, and so on.

You see, living inside our brains are quite a few different people.
Unfortunately, for most of the time, the most dominant person is
the guy who has to perform most of the time. You are in work mode
for a greater proportion of your waking hours and it is difficult to
shut off the stress and fully relax when you get the chance.

The picture I am painting is of a life that is full of often tedious routines, leaving us to ponder about what, if anything, we are really achieving.

When we take holidays, the other people inside us start to emerge and demand a new approach. Once we return to the routine, however, the old Mr or Mrs (or even Ms) dominant re-emerges. So, instead of waiting for that two- to four-week break per year to give your whole being a chance, why not do it every day?

My suggestion is very straightforward. Every day, spend around half an hour in some form of quiet time. In my opinion, meditation is the best form of quiet time – and I'll talk about that shortly – but it is not for everyone. Alternatives you might consider are relaxation tapes, listening to music, contemplating nature, engaging in a meditative hobby; I don't really care what it is, as long as you're sitting quietly. Not conversing, not reading, not watching television – just sitting.

MEDITATION

When you hear the word 'meditation', what image does it conjure? Most people in Western society think of a grey-haired Indian mystic with glazed eyes, wearing silk robes and speaking slowly. It is true that many of the masters of meditation do resemble this description, but it is also true that many successful, seemingly conservative people in Western society are embracing the technique and are experiencing its profound benefits. But before I describe the actual techniques involved, let's discuss the principles of meditation.

EGO AND SELF

There are two major components to self. Firstly, the higher self which is boundless and connected to the universal force and secondly the ego which defines us as a separate being. These two aspects are different although similar to the categorisation made by the father of psychiatry, Sigmund Freud, who divided the human condition into superego, ego and id. Freud saw the superego as our conscience, the ego as the external manifestation of our personality and the id as our basic drives, especially our sexual response.

I would prefer to examine our nature in more spiritual terms. If we are ruled by our ego we overstate our importance or in many cases understate our importance and the quality of our lives is judged by the day-to-day variability of our environmental experiences.

If, for example, your ego enjoys being the centre of attention, if you have a day when everything goes well and people are showering you with compliments, then you judge this as a good day. If, however, you have a day when there is criticism of your actions, you feel bad.

Wayne Dyer, the psychologist, author and spiritual teacher, tells a wonderful story. Because of his prominence as an author, he receives many letters commenting on and questioning his publications. In one day, he opened two letters about one of his books. The first letter said this particular book was the best book the person had ever read and it had changed his life forever. The second letter-writer, however, said the same book was the worst book they had ever read and they wanted their money back.

Rather than being upset about this, Dr Dyer, in his own unique and unaffected manner, photocopied both letters and sent them to the opposite readers. The first reader received the 'I want my money back' letter and the second reader received the life-changing letter. Dr Dyer's actions here are fascinating and work on a few levels. First, he was able to remove his own ego from the process. He did not bask in the glory of the praise, nor did he choose to defend himself against his detractor. Second, he very cleverly pointed out to both people involved that there is always an alternative interpretation to any situation, and in most situations neither opinion is superior, but is just that: an ego-based opinion.

Basically, our individual egos respond separately to each and every situation. Because our egos are so sensitive to these subtle and not-so-subtle changes in our environment, they are never really content or satisfied. We therefore create material experiences to pacify these ever-demanding egos.

From this constant desire for stimulation comes dissatisfaction and frustration. We see this so often, especially in children and younger people. If a child sees another child with a toy, they immediately want the toy. Teenagers now must wear designer label clothes otherwise they are not 'cool'. Now, unfortunately, with the availability of mature entertainment in television, videos/DVDs, computers and the internet, this alleged premature sophistication of children and teenagers means that they're having experiences well before their time and by the time they reach mid to late teens, their forever unsatisfied egos are crying out for more.

They are always searching for the ultimate experience, which continually eludes them. Unfortunately, their search now often leads them to seek answers through substance abuse, premature sexual experiences or other high-risk behavioural patterns – all to stimulate the never-satisfied ego. Who's to blame for allowing this to happen?

It is my opinion that the explosion of unchecked materialism has elevated the position of the ego to a level way beyond its rightful position. The reality is, if you look to the ego as your primary motivation, you will never be satisfied. All you can hope for is temporary, acute appeasement. Just think of a roller-coaster ride (and I must say I think this isn't a bad analogy for many of life's experiences). It's great fun and for many people very exciting but it's over in a few minutes and the thrill certainly doesn't last beyond the ride. Fortunately, however, the roller-coaster doesn't have too many long-term side effects, unless of course you are a sufferer of vertigo or are prone to throwing up during or after the ride.

Many of the experiences we seek as adults are just more sophisticated 'roller-coaster rides' but unfortunately many can have serious long-term consequences.

For example, the acute rush of a sexual encounter with someone other than your regular partner can not only have major health

issues, but can also jeopardise your more important primary relationship, especially if it drives you into long-term clandestine
behaviour. All this, purely for a new source of stimulation for that
forever-craving ego.

Excessive eating, alcohol abuse or uncontrolled spending are all
examples of the ego appeasement that is never successful. The
more fuel you throw on the fire, the more intensely it burns.

THE HIGHER SELF

If, however, you see your higher self as your primary motivational
force, you will experience a complete change of perspective and
achieve a peace and contentment that is impossible if you are living
in ego mode.

A major gateway to the higher self is through meditation.
Deepak Chopra, another spiritual teacher and physician, is a great
proponent of meditation. Dr Chopra attended medical school in
India before becoming an endocrinologist (a specialist in disorders
of hormones and metabolism) at ·Harvard University in America.
After practising endocrinology for a number of years, he became
fascinated with the mind–body connection, learning transcendental meditation from the Maharishi Mahesh Yogi (the guru who
taught the Beatles to meditate in the Sixties) and studied Ayurvedic
medicine, the ancient Indian art of healing.

He stopped formally practising Western medicine and
became a famous metaphysical author and world-renowned
speaker promoting the benefits of meditation and exploration of
the higher self.

Dr Chopra, in his many books and lecture series, discusses the
concept of silent intelligence. Silent intelligence is the 'God force'
which controls the universe. It is the force that directs our cells to
do the work, that makes a liver cell a liver cell or instructs a white
cell to rid the body of a virus or a bacteria. The silent intelligence
also directs the leaves to fall from the trees in autumn and to regrow

in spring. This is all done with a minimum of fuss and without an enormous effort. It just seems to happen.

When we meditate, we move into the space where this silent intelligence exists. It cannot be measured, seen, touched or smelt. It can, however, be felt.

The greatest motivating force on this Earth is not power, money or sex – all these are ego-based motivations. The greatest motivating force is love. Love emanates from this space and love cannot be measured, although not many people question love's existence. Our desire to practise and emanate unconditional love is greatly enhanced through meditation.

I'm not suggesting you cannot be an exponent of unconditional love without meditation, but learning this wonderful technique focuses your mind on the higher self, shifting you away from affairs of the ego.

TAPPING INTO THE 'GOD FORCE'

So, how do you move into the realm of this silent intelligence? First, it is important to understand the basic mechanisms of the mind. Every component of the conscious mind is based around the following fundamental concept. We start with a thought, which leads on to an idea, which culminates in an action. From the simple thought that my bladder is full, to an idea (not what I would call an amazing insight in this case), I will commit the necessary act and empty my bladder.

A more complex thought–idea–action plan would be one such as the sequence followed when working through a relationship problem. You have the thought of that person, then the idea of how that person is affecting your life and vice versa, then move on to a possible solution or action involving that person. This complex interactive sequence may take many hours of thought and rumination before an appropriate, or at times inappropriate, solution presents itself.

Every day our minds are processing these constant sequences of thoughts–ideas–actions, not allowing the higher self the necessary peace and calm for self-nurturing.

Meditation takes you to the place where thoughts arise – the silent gap between and before thoughts. So, the sequence really should read: pre-thought and then thought–idea–decision–action. There are many forms of meditation which have very similar results. I, personally, practise transcendental meditation. Which reminds me – have you heard about the Hindu guru who visited the dentist for a tooth extraction? When asked if he wanted local anaesthetic, he declined, stating he wanted to transcend dental medication!

TRANSCENDENTAL MEDITATION

Some years ago, a colleague of mine was undermining me, spreading rumours and smearing my reputation. He was making my life a misery to the point where I was no longer enjoying my work.

During this period, my life was reaching rock bottom and as the universe often directs, the head of the Australian Transcendental Meditation Foundation, who was leasing premises from me at the time, came to me with a proposal. He was going to teach me transcendental meditation.

This was exactly what I needed to regain my enthusiasm and zest for life. I have been practising this technique on a daily basis since that time.

THE TECHNIQUES OF TRANSCENDENTAL MEDITATION

Transcendental meditation involves the use of a mantra. A mantra is a phrase that has no significance or meaning at a superficial language level but the Hindus believe it is a mystical phrase that is the vehicle for connections to this silent gap.

Transcendental meditation is practised by sitting quietly in a comfortable place and repeating the mantra over and over inside your mind. You do not need to make the sound 'om', or sit cross-legged with your palms up and your thumb and forefinger making the shape of an O. You simply need to sit quietly and comfortably.

After a period of this repetition, your entire physiology slowly winds down and the global benefits begin. Of course, your busy brain will throw in many unwanted thoughts. Just picture this – it's early morning and you have settled down in your favourite chair to meditate. You are comfortable and you close your eyes. Within a few seconds, you bring in your mantra. After an indeterminate period, you lose the mantra and lapse into deep meditation, but then a thought appears, as if from nowhere.

'I've got that appointment at 9.30 am. I really don't like that person, they are so arrogant and will not listen to my – wait a minute, I'm supposed to be meditating.' So you bring your focus back to the mantra and soon return to this deep state. This scenario will be repeated throughout your meditation session but you will nevertheless achieve numerous bursts of deep and prolonged meditation that will have profound effects way beyond the session.

If, after reading this section, you are motivated to learn meditation, I strongly suggest you seek a meditation teacher. Although the technique is very simple, you will derive the greatest benefit through the guidance of an expert.

THE LASTING BENEFITS OF MEDITATION

So what does meditation do for you and how is it beneficial? Firstly and most obviously, meditation has a general calming effect that rests the body. This allows any accumulating stress to be released.

In a way, you should see stress like a rubbish bin. If the bin is not emptied regularly, the rubbish overflows and causes a mess. See the act of meditation as calling in the garbologist who empties the bin.

Meditation certainly does not stop the rubbish from re-accumulating but is an efficient means of clearing the rubbish once it is there.

No matter what you may read or hear from even the most convincing motivational speakers, we are all affected by stress and are all affected by life's ups and downs and by our own mistakes. Meditation is an excellent form of damage control to minimise the deleterious effects of ongoing stress. It's really a bit like taking Valium without the sedating effects.

But is this all meditation does? Certainly not! Meditation has profound physiological effects. We sleep to rejuvenate our bodies for the next day. After fourteen to sixteen waking hours, we need around eight hours for this process. Although it varies with age, for most adults around one to two hours of sleep are spent in what we call phase 4 non-REM sleep, which is the deep rejuvenating sleep, the so-called Delta rhythm.

It is during this phase that our pulse and breathing slows down, our brain waves are minimal and our system is in quiescence. Reparative systems kick in and hormones such as growth hormone and other protein-repairing chemicals help restore damaged or failing cells.

One half-hour of a deeper meditation can have the reparative effects of around four hours of sleep. Interestingly, these effects combined have profound long-term physical and psychological benefits. People who are regular meditators have 50 to 60 per cent less heart disease and cancer. People who meditate are generally much less stressed and happier, more effective people.

CASE STUDY – RANJIT

Ranjit Dev is a 46-year-old man who two years ago underwent a coronary artery stent for a tight blockage in the main artery in his heart. Ranjit unfortunately inherited a strong tendency for premature heart disease and was also working in a very stressful occupation as one of the top executives in a prominent insurance company.

> Although Ranjit was taking appropriate pills to lower his choles-
> terol, he was not following any correct lifestyle principles and despite
> his Indian heritage had never considered meditation. After his con-
> sultation with me, he decided to learn meditation and rearrange his
> dietary and exercise habits.

I was gratified to learn from Ranjit a few months later that he felt better than he had for years. He told me that his life had taken on an entirely new perspective.

The final point I would like to make regarding meditation is the most contentious. Either meditation is an excellent method of relaxation or it is more. If it is more, what is this more? Why did Ranjit feel that he had a new perspective? It is my belief that meditation is our transport to our higher self. The only other transport is prayer and some would rightly argue that meditation is a deep form of prayer.

For those of us who believe in a higher being or force, we cannot directly tap into that force without a vehicle. Meditation or prayer are the best vehicles to achieve this direct communication. These important modalities allow us to spend time in our higher self and realise the lesser place of the ego.

The perspective gained by living in a higher self puts us on purpose and opens our lives to a new, deeper, more rewarding way of existence.

2 LEAD A PRINCIPLE-CENTRED LIFE

Steven Covey wrote the book *The Seven Habits of Highly Effective People*. Of course, in my opinion Steve got it slightly wrong – it should have been the *five* habits. When will people realise – everything comes in fives!

Seriously, the major point of Steve's excellent book is that we should all live principle-centred lives. So many people centre their lives on their work, the acquisition of money and material goods and the worst focus of all – hatred or dislike for another human being, religion or country.

At a macrocosmic level, the world is presently in the grip of terrorist threats and actions because these groups hate the principles of Western society. At a microcosmic level, a human being who is consumed with hatred for another person is always a bent and twisted individual.

There is a wonderful Buddhist saying that clearly sums up this entire scenario: 'If you want to throw a hot coal at someone, remember you will burn your own hand first.'

Covey talks about being centred on your highest values and principles. If, in all your dealings, you aspire to simple principles such as truth, honesty, integrity and service to others, you'll be rapidly on the Life Factor path to inner peace and happiness.

Do not judge yourself or others by the size of their bank balance, their new car or house or their occupation. In fact, a very simple life principle is to work hard every day in your life not to judge anyone. Unfortunately, we all (including me) tend to judge. Why? Because, as we have seen, we have a rather large impediment following us around everywhere we go – it's called the ego.

3 NURTURE YOUR ATTITUDE

I've spoken earlier about Viktor Frankl and his simple but powerful statement, 'It's not the suffering, but the way you handle it, that's important.'

This straightforward principle can be applied to all aspects of life, both positive and negative. Learning to nurture your attitude is a key concept. Attitude encompasses many things. It can be your attitude to your appearance, your family, your wealth, your poverty, your pain, your pleasure – the list is endless. It is the dignity with which you handle every situation. It is your demeanour in regard to other people. My advice is to put in that conscious effort to change your attitude if you believe it is not serving you or those around you in the best possible manner.

SELF-DISCIPLINE

One of the key aspects of attitude is self-discipline. There are five important aspects of self-discipline:

- **(a)** delayed gratification
- **(b)** truth
- **(c)** responsibility
- **(d)** balance
- **(e)** will.

(a) Delayed gratification

Leading psychologist and frequently quoted author Daniel Goleman wrote the famous book *Emotional Intelligence*. In this book, he cites an important study conducted on a group of toddlers. One by one, these toddlers were taken into a room containing a table and a plate, and on that plate was a marshmallow. The toddlers were told that the researcher had to leave the room but if they could wait till he returned, they would get two marshmallows. If, however, they wanted only one, they could eat it immediately.

The toddlers' behaviour was observed. Fifteen years later, the children, now teenagers, were re-assessed. Those children who as toddlers had displayed the ability to delay gratification by waiting for the second marshmallow showed significant life differences compared with those who had eaten the marshmallow immediately.

The delayed gratification group were much more successful people. They had better scores on their final exams at high school, a lower percentage of crime and drug addiction and were generally happier when evaluated using psychological testing.

The simple, though at times difficult, ability to be able to wait or delay gratification is a vital step in self-discipline. This 'I want it and I want it now' attitude is a major feature of modern society and a central issue in our burgeoning divorce rates, credit card debts and substance abuse. If you are not already a 'delayed gratification-ist', learn the habit. It's actually not that difficult. The next time you feel like something you know is not all that good for you, delay con-suming, using, committing the act by at least fifteen minutes to half an hour. If you still feel like it (which you often won't) – go ahead. The more you discipline yourself to delay something, the easier it becomes.

(b) Truth

Seek a truthful explanation for everything, especially where you are involved. If, for example, one of your goals is weight loss, this is a situation where self-discipline is vitally important. Why are you overweight? Tell the truth. I have many people with significant weight problems who tell me they eat like a sparrow. I live in fear of one of those sparrows flying over my head at the wrong time!

If I detained one of these 'sparrow eaters' in a draconian prison camp and fed them minimal food, I can assure you this non-nourishment would rapidly lead to their losing weight.

It is not big bones or genetics that can be directly blamed for an excess of weight – it is the oculo-salivary reflex! The old 'seefood diet'; they see food and they eat it!

(c) Responsibility

Following close on the heels of truth is responsibility. Don't go blaming other people, genetics, glands and so on for your problems. Take control, take responsibility. Once you're firmly in charge of your own destiny, you then will take steps to change.

(d) Balance

I will discuss balance in full in the final section of this chapter. Suffice to say, a vital component of self-discipline is balance.

Buddhists commonly refer to the 'Middle Path'. This is, in reality, seeking balance in all things – a major theme of this book. To follow the 'Middle Path' requires and enhances self-discipline.

(e) *Will*

Great champions in any field have a strong desire to achieve. This desire leads to a vital component of success. The self-reliance movement essentially began in the 1930s with the release of Napoleon Hill's book *Think and Grow Rich*. In it, he discusses the factors that create success. One of the major factors he identified when examining the lives of successful people was perseverance. If you want something enough, never give up. If your first attempts don't work, formulate a new plan and persevere until you are successful. Without the will or desire, however, there is little likelihood your plans will succeed.

The famous psychologist Abraham Maslow describes the 'no limit' person. This person has three important characteristics that I believe are principles to which we should all aspire:

- ▸ Be independent of the good opinion of other people – don't judge your own life based on others' opinions. Don't try to blend into the crowd. Follow your own beliefs if they accord with your higher values.
- ▸ Stay detached from the outcome. Whatever you are involved in, enjoy the act, not the result. Don't help someone because there might be something in it for you. We all work to earn an income but perform your job with interest, spirit and enthusiasm no matter what the task and I guarantee you will reap results.
- ▸ Have no desire to have power over others. Many of our day-to-day activities, whether at home or at work, are power plays between people. One of the important principles of a happy and successful life is 'try to be kind, rather than right'.

APPRECIATE THE PATH YOU'RE ON

Whilst I am writing this book, I am literally sitting on a beach in Bali with the ocean waves lapping around 10 metres away. It is a beautiful, sunny day and a warm gentle breeze is blowing across my body. Sounds idyllic? It is! So, is writing this book a means to an end? No, it is an end in itself.

One of the greatest learning methods is to have to teach someone else – to do so effectively you must really make sure you know what you're talking about. The research for this book, the preparation and subsequent writing have all been an enriching, learning experience for me. This book is, in many ways, the culmination of years of treating patients, interacting with all manner of people, and my own life journey. I have had many privileges, including delivering lectures to thousands of people throughout the globe, and these entire experiences of living, writing, lecturing and practising medicine have certainly allowed me to appreciate the path. Whatever you do, learn to appreciate the path also.

If you have stumbled on to a path that is causing you grief, use the steps set out in this book to change that path. Redirect yourself to a more rewarding, more empowering, more enjoyable path.

4 QUESTION THE THINKING–FEELING CONNECTION

Throughout our lives we have formulated many opinions, beliefs and reactions to stimuli based on our particular experiences. When we live in our 'default' mode, we are usually reactive rather than proactive. Once we have experienced a situation, we formulate an opinion about that situation, which is usually linked to an emotion. That emotion has been formed based on our experience of the situation. This emotion may be very destructive and, if not dealt with, creates problems for many years to come.

For example, if you were abused as a child at any level, your relationships as an adult may be dictated by the level of abuse you received at the hands of the abuser.

This thinking–feeling connection may make it very difficult for you to form proper relationships as an adult. Whilst many other people derive emotional gratification from their relationships, you may live in lifelong torment because of your inability to develop proper, fulfilling relationships.

Fortunately, modern psychology has developed many novel, effective techniques to deal with this. All these techniques have a common thread; they break the old thinking–feeling connection and replace it with a new connection.

To do so, you must move outside your comfort zone to prevent the old default mechanisms creeping back in and creating those ingrained aberrant reactions.

To be effective in this regard, you must learn to nurture your imagination. Fantasy is the creation of a novel, as yet unachieved, situation. To make your fantasy a reality, to turn a fear into a pleasure, a dream into a realised goal, practise visualisation. Sit quietly for at least five minutes per day with your eyes closed, visualising that you have achieved your desire or goal. Visualise in the present tense.

There are two types of changes you may want to make:

▶ a positive, new behaviour or situation that you wish to gain
▶ a negative, old behaviour or situation that you desire to lose.

With the first, associate present, vivid and colourful change with strong positive emotions. You will realise your goal. With the second, associate past, distant visualisations in drab black and white. You will make this unwanted behaviour neutral emotionally by using this technique.

Many great thinkers have been strong visualisers. Albert Einstein first thought of his theory of relativity by imagining he was travelling on a beam of light with a hand mirror. He visualised that he would still be able to see his face in the mirror despite travelling at the speed of light, thereby knocking a rather large hole in New-tonian physics – purely through the technique of visualisation. I discussed visualisation techniques in chapter 6, so turn to that chapter if you'd like to refresh your memory. For those of you interested in pursuing this topic further, there is a large body of work known as neurolinguistic programming, which explores in depth the practical use of these procedures.

5 AIM FOR BALANCE

Throughout this book I highlight the importance of having a balanced life. In our modern world we constantly struggle to achieve this balance.

The famous Australian painter Brett Whiteley was a genius. Unfortunately, the operative word is 'was', because he is now dead. He packed so much living into his 45 years, so much more than most of us would manage in a lifetime. But did he live a happy and fulfilled life? I think not. He was struggling to attain something more.

CASE STUDY – GEORGE

George Watkins is 43 years old. He wakes up every morning at 6.45 am. He empties his bladder and then does five minutes of stretching exercises before he has his cereal, two pieces of toast and a cup of decaf coffee with no milk and reads the morning paper. At precisely 7.45 am he walks the ten minutes from his house to the train station. He catches the 7.57 am train and arrives in the city at 8.46 am. Every weekday morning he is in the office by 8.58 am. He has the neatest desk in the office. He is efficient, a diligent worker and is quite popular in his workplace. He leaves at 5.02 pm every day, reading the evening paper on the way home.

> He is always the first to volunteer to organise a farewell for the next retiree. He runs the office Christmas club and has never had a cross word with anyone. Each year, he and his wife, Doreen, visit the same place for holidays. They have, of course, two children; a boy and a girl. They used the ovulation method to ensure they had a pigeon pair. George is the coach of his son's soccer team and referees his daughter's netball and is no doubt on the soccer and netball chocolate wheel at the local school fete. He visits his ailing mother in the nursing home every Tuesday night and Sunday morning. Nothing really seems to faze him. His life is completely ordered. He certainly never hits rock bottom, but let's face it, he never reaches any peaks either.

George Watkins and Brett Whiteley are two absolutely different human beings. One has left a mark on society at a great personal price and the other will probably never leave a major mark on society but is nevertheless an important contributing member, almost like a foundation stone or a yardstick against which the flamboyant in society can be judged.

What basic thread are we discussing here? It is obviously the theme of balance. Both of these characters lack the balance that is needed to truly enjoy life. Maybe Mr Whiteley did enjoy his wild swings between pleasure and pain. Maybe our friend George does enjoy his very ordered (some would say extremely boring) existence. But is there a compromise here, is there a balance? I believe the answer is yes.

To achieve balance in our lives, we need to do work in five main categories:

(a) physical
   ‣ nutrition (including alcohol intake and supplementation)
   ‣ exercise and movement
   ‣ no smoking
   ‣ achieving quality sleep
   ‣ appropriate preventative check-ups

(b) mental
(c) emotional
(d) financial
(e) spiritual.

(a) PHYSICAL BALANCE

An ancient and very wise philosopher once said, 'If you ain't got your health, you got nothing.'

Simple, but true. You may spend your life accumulating wealth, knowledge, caring, nurturing relationships and intense spiritual wisdom, but if you die prematurely you cannot really feel that these acquisitions along the way were particularly worthwhile. In fact, you cannot say or feel anything, because you're dead.

Achieving balance in your physical self is therefore vital for the maintenance of balance in all other aspects. I have extensively covered the topic of physical balance in my other books and have also discussed aspects of these issues throughout this book.

Achieving quality sleep

The only area not already covered to any great depth, however, is that of sleep. Many people, for many varied reasons, sleep very poorly. In my Life Program, I deliver a lecture entitled 'How to Achieve Perfect Sleep'. This is such a large topic that I could not possibly do it justice in a few lines. I will, however, give a brief summary of the major points of my lecture advice regarding achieving better sleep.

Good-quality sleep is vital for normal day-to-day functioning. I firmly believe that the way you feel and behave tomorrow depends on how you sleep tonight. The functions of sleep are therefore to:

▸ rejuvenate, repair and rest
▸ maintain the normal sleep–wakefulness balance
▸ contribute to normal circadian rhythm.

Some people see sleep as a waste of time; others consider it a wonderful indulgence. Regardless, sleep is a vital physiological function allowing these three major aspects of our normal metabolism to occur.

The quality of your sleep depends on the following five factors:

(i) quality of your waking hours
(ii) preparation for sleep
(iii) sleeping environment
(iv) quality of sleep
(v) 24-hour cycle.

The quality of your waking hours very much depends on your ability to manage your life – which is precisely the topic of this book. The major determinants of your waking hours (apart from sleep quality itself) are:

▸ nutrition
▸ fitness
▸ work habits
▸ underlying illnesses
▸ personal psychological state.

Preparing and planning for sleep is very important, just as it is important to plan for all other aspects of your life. In preparing for sleep there are two major considerations – the activities that you should avoid, and the activities that are helpful.

Activities to avoid are:

▸ family/ emotional problems (including phone calls) – one hour before sleep
▸ exercise – two hours before sleep
▸ eating – two hours before sleep
▸ alcohol/stimulants/other drugs – three hours before sleep.
▸ falling asleep in front of the television/radio or with a light on.

Activities to encourage are:

▸ reading a magazine/novel – half an hour before sleep
▸ warm bath/shower – one hour before sleep
▸ warm non-caffeine-based drink – one hour before sleep
▸ relaxation tapes/CD – just before sleep
▸ lovemaking.

Your *sleeping environment* is important. Feng Shui practitioners are always very interested in this aspect of our physical surroundings.

I will make some comments now that might seem heretical. I believe that the bedroom is for sleeping and lovemaking and for little else. I believe the television should be banned from the bedroom. There should not be other electronic gadgets such as computers/fax machines, and so on. Try to make your bedroom as comforting and enticing an environment as possible.

A vital part of good sleep is a comfortable bed with comfortable pillows. Beds that are too firm or too soft can cause problems, depending on the individual's needs.

Another vital aspect of the sleeping environment is the person next to you, if indeed you sleep with someone. A poor relationship, a restless sleeper, a snorer or someone with a chronic illness who is either coughing, endlessly waking up to pass urine (hopefully not in the bed), or some other concerning complaint, can also disrupt your sleep.

What is going on outside the bedroom can be just as disrupting as inside the bedroom. A barking dog, noisy neighbours or traffic noise can create enormous disturbances.

Other disruptions that are in many ways necessary and unavoidable, such as crying or sick children, are great sleep killers.

The *quality of sleep* itself is important. Try following the five 'R's of sleep:

▸ Routine – going to sleep around the same time each night is important for quality sleep.

▸ Relaxed – probably the strongest sleep killer is going to bed stressed. Try sleeping after a screaming argument with a family member or during an intense period of work disruption. It just won't happen.

▸ Reducing temperature – the function of the warm bath or shower or warm drink is the after-effect of reducing temperature. It is much harder to sleep if your body temperature is rising.

▸ Relationship – poor relationships often equate with poor sleep. In my medical practice, the greatest complaints of poor sleep come from the people involved in long-term domestic problems or work stress.

▸ Ready – your body knows when it needs sleep. Don't go to bed and try to sleep if you are wide awake.

The *24-hour cycle* is always a factor. Our body clocks are constantly ticking away. These clocks give us our circadian rhythms and time our cellular mechanisms (if we let them), to perfection. Sleep is a key component of this 24-hour cycle. Most studies suggest that somewhere between six to eight hours is the ideal amount of sleep for most adults, certainly decreasing as you age.

(b) MENTAL BALANCE

The average lifespan of a Detroit executive following retirement, in one particular study, was around one year. If you stop using what Hercule Poirot called 'those little grey cells', they stop working.

Like any organ in the body, our brain cells need constant stimulation and challenge. Sure, there are some people who appear particularly gifted and seem to have the edge over the majority of people with average intelligence.

Strangely, the brain of the twentieth century's greatest mind, that of Albert Einstein, is now sitting in a jar in a Kansas university. His brain has been studied extensively and although it is no larger than average, it has much richer connections. Most brain researchers believe these connections are formed through the process of thinking. Certainly they do not appear to be present to this degree at birth.

We therefore ask ourselves the important question: can we improve our intellect and thinking processes during our adult life, or is life a slowly progressive downhill intellectual roller-coaster? Einstein's now-deceased but well-studied brain would suggest the former. Einstein was a very active thinker, using all aspects of his thinking apparatus to formulate his works of genius.

The strong point I'm trying to make here is that we should be constantly using and nurturing this wonderful organ – our brain. Challenge your mind as much as possible. Use it or lose it. You should see every day as an opportunity for learning.

I hear so many people make comments like, 'School was useless, I didn't learn a thing' or, 'I don't know why I would bother, learning this stuff will be of no use to me whatsoever.' Often the people who make these comments are the same ones who don't mind sitting for hours in front of television, learning nothing and completely wasting their time!

A recent study has shown that the simple habit of regularly performing brain puzzles or doing a crossword improves longevity and brain function. There has never been a study suggesting the same results from watching television.

I'm not suggesting television should not be a part of your life but am certainly suggesting it should not occupy a central role. Balance in your mental development is vital. Do not induce information overload and work your grey cells to the point of exhaustion. On the other hand, the grey cells must be worked. Here are just some of many ways you can improve your intellect as you progress through this wonderful existence:

> ▸ *Learn to work with both sides of your brain.* Our society, in
>   many ways, places greater value on left-brain thinking
>   involving linguistic and mathematical intelligences.

Integrating right-brain techniques into your thinking processes enhances your global intelligence. One of the lectures I give is on advanced brain power and there are now a number of publications on how to improve your right-brain thinking.

▸ *Work with your subconscious mind.* The subconscious is an enormously untapped resource which needs to be developed.

▸ *Creative techniques.* There is a long list of creative techniques that can enhance your thinking. One simple example is the different types of classical music that can enhance your ability to learn.

▸ *Preparation for learning.* This involves two important areas: firstly, a clear purpose for your learning activity and secondly, achieving the correct brain state for learning.

▸ *Accelerated learning techniques.* Rather than the old methods of didactic teaching, there are now a number of accelerated methods which make learning easier and more enjoyable.

The above is only a very brief overview of the topic. It deserves a book in itself – in fact, it is the basis of a full-day seminar I present on advanced brain power.

(c) EMOTIONAL BALANCE

Emotional balance is achieved by having balance, not only in your close relationships, but also in all other areas of your life.

In the previous chapter, I talked about how you can achieve balance in your relationships. It is important to stress that you also need to strive for emotional balance by achieving balance in your physical, mental, financial and spiritual side.

Treating your body poorly will lead to an imbalance in your emotions. Lack of fitness, constant fatigue, or chronic illnesses typically lead to irritability, anxiety and other disordered emotional states.

Mental frustration through poor memory, concentration and other aspects of inadequate learning often leads to emotional imbalance. Overwhelming financial problems are a common cause of emotional instability and disharmony.

Finally, a lack of spiritual balance may lead to chronic emotional issues. Lack of meaning in our lives can often be the source of emotional discontent.

(d) FINANCIAL BALANCE

Although money cannot buy you happiness, not having it will often create unhappiness. I must, however, state one important piece of financial advice that will hold you in good stead for the rest of your days: never ask a doctor for financial advice. I do believe it is important to surround yourself with experts. I rely heavily on my financial planner and accountant to help me manage my finances because I'm not so good at doing so myself.

(e) SPIRITUAL BALANCE

Although religion appears to be a major player in many of the world's conflicts, as I said earlier, I don't believe we can blame God for that. Conscious contact with a higher spiritual force does give life meaning and balance.

My only comment is – and I have no right to set myself up as an expert in this area – follow the philosophy with which you're most comfortable.

ACTION SUMMARY

If you are unhappy with your current circumstances, then why don't you make the decision to change. In this chapter, I have suggested some different approaches which you may find are important instruments to bring about these changes.

Albert Einstein once said, 'There is nothing that is a more certain sign of insanity than to do the same thing over and over and expect the results to be different.'

Change now, because if you don't, nothing will ever change. Don't just read this book and then set it aside and maintain your current existence. The people in our world who make a difference in their own lives and the lives of others are always those who refuse to go with the flow. Gandhi, Rosa Parks, Mother Teresa, to name a few, saw something they didn't like and decided to change it. Each was an individual with one voice and one mind. That's all any of us have. It is my firm belief that we are all in a position to change what we don't like at any level – we just have to really want it enough. In this book, I've given you the means; now it's up to you to achieve the end.

Further reading

de Bono, Edward, *Serious Creativity*, HarperCollins, London, 1996

Chopra, Deepak, *Quantum Healing*, Bantam Books, New York, 1990

Clason, George S., *The Richest Man in Babylon*, Penguin Books, New York, 1991

Covey, Steven, *The Seven Habits of Highly Effective People*, The Business Library, Melbourne, 1993

Dyer, Wayne, *Manifest Your Destiny: There is a Spiritual Solution to Every Problem*, HarperCollins, Sydney, 1997

Frankl, Vicktor E., *Man's Search for Meaning*, Beacon Press, Boston, 1959

Goleman, Daniel, *Emotional Intelligence*, Bantam Books, New York, 1995

Gray, John, *Men Are From Mars, Women Are From Venus*, HarperCollins, London, 1992

Hill, Napoleon, *Think and Grow Rich*, Ballantine Books, New York, 1988

Kubler-Ross, Elizabeth, *On Death and Dying*, Macmillan, London, 1969

Myss, Caroline, *Anatomy of the Spirit*, Crown Publishers, New York, 1996

—— *Sacred Contracts*, Crown Publishers, New York, 2001

Satir, Virgina, *Conjoint Family Therapy*, Science and Behaviour Books, California, 1983

Tolle, Eckhart, *The Power of Now: A Guide to Spiritual Enlightenment*, New World Library, California, 1999

Yalom, Irvin D., *Love's Executioner and Other Tales of Psychotherapy*, Penguin Books, London, 1991

Index

abdominal pain   77, 82
abreaction   77
acceptance   46, 156
accidents, road   20
acetylcholine   15
activities, dangerous   16
acute stress   150–1
   benefit from   156–7
   confronting   151–2
   dealing with   150–7
   five stages of grief   154–6
   taking action   153–4
   see also stress
Adams, Douglas   55
addictions   16–17, 76, 132, 174
   creating new patterns   137–44
   as escape hatch   112, 120,
      123–7
   physical   127
   pleasure-seeking   126–7
   rituals   125–6, 130
   withdrawal symptoms   131
adrenal glands   3
adrenaline   14, 15, 85
adrenaline seekers   16
affirmations   95, 138

ageing
   attitude to   44–5
   fear of   35, 44–8
aggression   67
agoraphobia   36–7, 121
alcohol   24, 131
alcoholics, parental love   61
Alison (elderly patient)   31–2,
   145–6
amygdala   113
ancient man   12, 15
Angela (case study)   73–4
anger   73, 154–5
   escape hatch   112–14, 120
   and grief   84
anticipation   144, 145–6
antidepressants   85
anxiety   83, 120–1
   and choice   17, 50
anxiety attacks   38–9
arterial tonometry   79
association (of thoughts)   146
atheism   57
attention deficit disorder (ADD)
   189–91
attitude nurturing   202–6

self-discipline 203–5
attraction 170
Australian Transcendental
  Meditation Foundation 198
autonomic nervous system
  12–15, 16
awareness 9, 11, 19, 70

balance, in life 24, 27, 34, 72,
  163, 208–9
  emotional balance 210,
    215–16
  financial balance 210, 216
  mental balance 210, 213–15
  physical balance 209, 210–13
  spiritual balance 210, 216
bargaining 155
basic needs 15, 46
beauty 28, 29, 171
behaviour
  adrenaline-inducing 16
  enjoyable 142
  high-risk 37, 133, 195
  ritual 121
benzodiazepines 82
black sheep 61
blood-brain barrier 190
bodily functions 112
body clock 213
bonding
  in groups 99
  mother-child 50, 65–6
  partners 177
brain 12, 16, 25, 55–6, 190, 214
  amygdala 113
  brainstem 112
  child's 61
  frontal lobes 113
  function 85
  left/right 112, 214–15

male/female differences 182–4
  midbrain 112
  neo-cortex 112
  occipital area 113
  parietal lobes 113
  regions 112
  structure 112–13
  temporal lobes 113
brain cells 25–6, 213, 214
brain chemistry 24
breaks, from work 160–1
breath, shortness of 77
Buddhism 114, 202
  Middle Path 205
bureaucracy 20–1

cancer 24, 28, 41, 86, 124
  and meditation 200
Cane, Rodney 140
cardiovascular symptoms 122–3
career change 103–4
case studies
  Angela 73–4
  Con Marcos 135–6
  Daniel 69
  Don 71
  Eric and Rosemary 53–4
  George Watkins 208–9
  Jeanette 124
  Julie and Stephen 51–2
  Karen 72
  Kim Napier 133–4
  Larry 78–9
  Leon 60–1
  Marcus 74–5
  Pam 126
  Peter Princeton 46–8
  Phil 73
  Ranjit Dev 200–1
  Robert Wilson 117–18

Rodney Cane 140
self-concept 62
Sheehan family 63–4
Terry 181
Trent and Diane 172–3, 174
catecholamines 85
cavemen 15
Cell Factor, The (Walker) 94, 95, 164
cellulite 94
cellulitis 133–4
change 20, 217
deciding to 127, 128–9
pace of 19–20
character 63, 65, 167
chest pain 77, 123
child abuse 31, 121, 176, 178, 181
childhood, early 59–70, 167
defective 73, 180
ego 61
encouragement 63
life experiences 65, 67–70
role models 61, 63, 65–6
children
frustrated 195
overstimulated 191
responsibility for 171, 172
Children's Medical Research Foundation 40
choice, overabundance of 17–18, 50, 192
Chopra, Deepak 196
cigarette smoking *see* smoking
cirrhosis, of liver 134
clairvoyance 55
Coffs Harbour, NSW 31
cognitive behavioural therapy (CBT) 84, 86
Cologne Cathedral, Germany 29
communication, instant 18

communication skills 184–5
companionship 52
conditioning, new patterns 144–6
confidence 66
conflicts 9
confrontation 153
Confucius 107
conscious mind 197
consciousness 11, 35
constipation 77
consumerism 31
contact, human 52
contemplation 18–19
contrasts 10
control 33
coping mechanisms, bad 111–12, 113, 120
action plan to get rid of 127–48
coping mechanisms, good 147–9
action plan to establish 149–64
coronary artery bypass grafting 86
corporate culture 158
counselling 84, 86, 152
Covey, Steven 201–2
cravings 125, 132
crises 175
CT scanning 79

Daniel (case study) 69
de Bono, Dr Edward 97–8, 99, 160
six thinking hats 160
death 46, 57
fear of 35–44
of loved one 39–43, 75, 83, 86, 151, 175

of parent 68
decision 9–10, 33, 70
  and bad coping mechanisms
    127, 128–9
  in goal-setting 93–5
decision-making 129
decluttering life 162–3
dementia 28
denial 155
depression 83–6, 155–6
  endogenous (chemical) 83,
    84–6
  reactive 83–4
  signs 86
deprivation 105
Dev, Ranjit 200–1
development, personal 65–70
  gender 65, 67
  life experiences 65, 67–70
  position in family 65, 66–7
  role models 65–6
devotion 43
diabetes 72
diarrhoea 77
Dientamoeba fragilis 78
diet programs 105
diplomacy 153
discipline
  parental 190–2
  to condition new pattern
    144–5
discomfort 127, 135
disease 23, 24
  investigations 80–1
  prevention 92, 95
  resemblance to stress 78–80
diversity, of human behaviour
  180–4
divorce 68, 155
dizziness 77

Dodds, Jack 39–40
Dodds, Sir Lorimer 39–40
Don (case study) 71
dopamine 15, 16, 130
driving (car) 20, 113
drug abuse 28, 66, 131
drug addiction 61, 123–7, 133
Dyer, Wayne 194
dying 55

eating 30–1
Edison, Thomas 44, 116
ego 119, 193–6, 197, 201, 202
Einstein, Albert 9, 207–8, 217
  brain 213–14
electroconvulsive therapy (ECT)
  85–6
email 19
emotional balance 210, 215–16
emotional energy 23, 27–8
emotional goals 92, 101
Emotional Intelligence (Goleman)
  203
endogenous (chemical) depression
  83, 84–6
endorphins 15, 130, 147
endoscopy 81
energy 22–3, 158
  emotional 23, 27–8, 34
  mental 23, 24–7, 34
  nurturing 34
  physical 23–4, 34
  sensual 23, 29–32, 34
  spiritual 23, 32–4
  transfer of 34
  universal 23
energy levels 92, 94–5
envy 112, 117–19, 120
Eric and Rosemary (case study)
  53–4

escape hatches *see* coping
  mechanisms
exercise   24, 147
  program   94
extended family   52

familiarity   20, 173
families   27–8
  child's position in   65, 66–7
  dysfunctional   61–5, 68–70
  extended   52
  sibling relationships   68
  teenagers   68, 195
  see also children
Family Therapy (Satir)   62
fantasy   207
fear–flight/fight system   13–14,
  37, 123
fears   35, 36
  ageing   35, 44–8
  death   35–44
  flying   39
  freedom   35, 49–50
  heights   36
  isolation   35, 50–5
  lack of meaning   35, 55–8
  venturing out   36–7
feedback   109
Field, Sally   122
fight or flight response   13–14,
  37, 123
financial balance   210, 216
financial goals   92, 102
fitness   23, 92, 94
FLECA approach, to problem-
  solving   98, 100
flying, fear of   39
focus   19, 189, 191
follow-up   107
food   15, 22, 30–1

forgiveness   84, 119, 153, 185
Frankl, Viktor   33, 44, 202
freedom, fear of   35, 49–50
Freud, Sigmund   194
friendship   27
  with partner   177
frontal lobes, of brain   113
fulfilment   179
funeral eulogy   42

gastrointestinal problems   77,
  79–80, 120
gender   67
gluttony   30–1
goal-setting   91–110, 129
  action plan   103–10
  emotional goals   92, 101
  financial goals   92, 102
  mental goals   92, 100–1
  physical goals   92–100
  process   93–100
  spiritual goals   92, 102
goals   139
  daily review   106–7
  small steps   107
  time frame   129
God force   196, 197–8
God/higher being   55, 57, 102,
  169–70, 201
Goleman, Daniel   203
Grand Canyon, Arizona   29
grandparents   52, 68
gratification, delayed   203
Gray, John   180
greatness   40, 42
grief, stages   83–4, 154–6
group membership   98–9
growth, personal   43, 115, 116, 177
  and freedom   186
guilt   84

habits 49–50, 100, 144, 146
Harvard University, goal-setting
  study 91
headaches 77, 122
health, maintaining 24
health tailoring (Strecher) 131
hearing 29, 30, 108
heart, and stress 122–3
heart attack 78–9, 124, 142
  and personality 113–14
heart disease 24, 79, 116, 127
  and meditation 200
heart-rate monitor 94
heartbeat, rapid 123
heights, fear of 36
heroin 16, 127, 132
high-risk behaviour 37, 133, 195
higher being 55, 57, 102,
  169–70, 201
higher self 193, 196–7, 201
Hill, Napoleon 205
Hinduism 198
Hitchhiker's Guide to the Galaxy,
  The (Adams) 55
hoarseness 77
holidays 161–2, 192, 193
hopelessness 66
humanism 57
humour 163
hunter-gatherer society 15
hyperventilation 77
hypochondria 80–1
hypoxia 56
hysteria 121–2

id 194
imagination 108, 143, 207
immaturity 119
immune system 38
imperfection 10

inadequacy 10
infidelity 117–19, 174–5
information overload 214
instant answers, need for 18–19
intellect, improving 100, 214–15
intelligence, silent 196–7
intelligent questioning 139–41,
  156
interactions, approach to 168–9
irritable bowel syndrome 77–8
isolation 53
  fear of 35, 50–5

Janice (fear of flying) 39
jealousy 112, 117–19
Julie and Stephen (case study)
  51–2
Jung, Carl 121

Karen (case study) 72
King, Martin Luther 91
Kipling, Rudyard 140
knowledge acquisition 25
Kübler-Ross, Elizabeth 83–4,
  154

LA Story 192
language, internal 115, 169
Larry (case study) 78–9
lateral thinking 97–8
learning 25, 100–1, 214
  accelerated techniques 215
  new skills 96
  preparing for 215
left brain 112, 214
leisure 23
Leon (case study) 60–1
life
  healthy 24
  journey 46

lessons of   157
living in the moment   43, 189
meaning of   55–8, 102, 192
purpose   56, 102
quality of   29
reaction to   33
simplifying   57, 162–3
see also balance, in life
life expectancy   45
Life Journal   95, 106, 129
Life of Brian, The   165
light, solar   22
litigation   20, 154
loneliness   52, 53
loss   46, 154
love
romantic   170, 172, 173
unconditional   27, 33, 34, 43,
197
loved ones
death of   39–43, 75, 83, 86,
151, 175
neglected   101
loyalty   43

Macleod, Jeanette   124
malnourishment   23
Man's Search for Meaning (Frankl)
33
mantra   198
Marcos, Con   135–6
Marcus (case study)   74–5
marijuana   28
Martin, Steve   192
Maslow, Abraham   205
'no limit' person   205
massage   32
materialism   45, 195
meaning, of life   55–8, 102, 192
medical defence   20

meditation   14, 193, 196, 197,
198
benefits   199–201
higher self   193, 196–7
transcendental   198–9
meetings   159–60
de Bono's six thinking hats
160
memory aids   105
mental balance   210, 213–15
mental development   101
mental energy   23, 24–7
mental goals   92, 100–1
mentoring   109
mid-life crisis   99
midbrain   112
migraine   122
mind
conscious   197
subconscious   95, 107, 108,
139, 152, 215
morphine   16
mortality   10, 35, 55
motherhood   66, 183–4
motor vehicle accidents   20
motorists, and anger   20, 113
Mozart, WA   30
multi-skilling   19
multiple personalities   122
muscle tone   92, 94
music   30
Myss, Caroline   49, 185

Napier, Kim   133–4
nature, sounds of   30
nature-nurture debate   37
near-death experiences   55
neck problems   122
needs, basic   15, 46
negativity   100

as escape hatch 112, 115–17, 120
negotiation 155
neo-cortex 112
neurolinguistic programming (NLP) 135, 208
neuroses 36, 74, 120–2
neurotransmitters 15, 26, 85
nicotine addiction 123–6, 130–1
noradrenaline 14, 15, 85
novelty 143, 147, 173
nursing homes 45
nutrition 23, 24, 190

obsessive-compulsive neroses 121
occipital area, of brain 113
oesophageal pain 77
opiates 16
optimism 115, 116
overpopulation 45
oxygen 23, 33
    lack of 56

pain 26, 71–2, 189
    abdomen 77, 82
    chest 77, 123
    face 77
    oesophagus 77
palpitations 77, 120
Pam (case study) 126
panic attacks 38–9, 83, 121
paranormal events 55–6
parasympathetic nervous system 13, 14–15
parent, death of 68
parenting 59–70
    constancy 59, 61
    discipline 190–2
    encouragement 63

love 59, 61
    parents' issues 67
    positivity 63
    role models 61, 63, 167
    time costs 158
parietal lobes, of brain 113
Pascal, Blaise 19
passion 170, 173–4, 178–9
patterns
    limiting 129–37
    new 137–44
peace, inner 34
people skills 116
perceptions 61
    defective 9
perseverance 205
personalities, multiple 122
personality 52, 73, 167, 184
    type A/B 113–14
    type C 114
pessimism 115
Peter Pan syndrome 48
pheromones 30
Phil (case study) 73
philosophy 32–3, 44
phobias 36–7, 39, 83, 121
physical balance 209, 210–13
physical energy 23–4
physical goals 92–100
    disease prevention 92, 95
    energy levels 92, 94–5
    fitness 92
    ideal weight 92
    muscle tone 92
pins and needles 78
planning
    for goal achievement 139–42
    for goal-setting 96–9
pleasure 126, 135, 142
pleasure-pain reversal 134–7, 142

pleasure-reward-motivation system
  12, 15–17
  hyperstimulation of 16
pneumonia 86
Poirot, Hercule 213
positivity 63, 163
possessiveness 117, 176
Power of Now, The (Tolle) 189
power play 205
prayer 201
Princeton, Peter 46–8
principle-centred living 201–2
problem-solving 116
  de Bono's six thinking hats 98
  FLECA approach 98, 100
procreation 15, 178
progress, monitoring 109
psychiatric disorders 120
psychoses 120
public speaking 30, 105
pulse rate, measuring 94
purpose, of existence 56, 102
  see also meaning of life

quality of life 29
quality sleep 210–13
questioning, intelligent 139–41,
  156
quiet time 160, 193

rage 20, 113
rationalism 56, 57
reactive depression 83–4
reading 25, 101, 191
reductionism 56
reflection 19
reinforcement 107, 146–7
rejuvenation 13, 14–15, 23, 37–8
relationship breakdown 166,
  170–6

life crises 175
  ongoing problems 176
  personal baggage 175–6
  responsibility 171–3
  routine 173–5
relationships 50–1, 166, 168–9,
  180
  action plan 179–87
  affairs 16, 117–19, 174–5,
    195–6
  family 167
  friends 167–8, 180
  higher being 169–70
  improving 102
  parent-child 28, 32, 180–1
  primary partner 27, 166–7,
    170–1, 177–9
  siblings 68
  thinking-feeling connection
    207
  and touch 32
relaxation 14, 24, 100
relaxation/rejuvenation system
  13, 14–15, 37–8
religion 32, 33, 56, 170
reminder cards 95, 103
resentment 153
responsibility
  of older child 67
  in relationship breakdown
    171–3
  shared with partner 178
retirement dream 68
retirement syndrome 53–4
revenge 153–4
rewards 105
Richest Man in Babylon, The
  (Clason) 102
right brain 112, 215
risks, of new behaviour 99

rituals 125–6, 130, 144, 145
road rage 20, 113
role models 61, 63, 176
 female 65–6
 male 65, 66
routines 49–50, 100, 147

Sanders, Colonel 115
Satir, Virginia 62, 70
schizophrenia 56, 69
science 55–6
security 20
self-awareness 9, 11, 19, 70
self-care 163–4, 169
self-development 163–4
self-discipline 203–5
 balance 203, 204–5
 delayed gratification 203
 responsibility 203, 204
 truth 203, 204
 will 203, 205
self-improvement 10, 100, 169
self-monitoring 109
self-talk 115, 169
 positive 139, 155
self-worth 52
sensory system (five senses) 29, 108
sensual energy 23, 29–32
separation 68
serotonin 85, 86
service, to others 33, 34, 102
Seven Habits of Highly Effective People, The 201–2
sexual satisfaction 178–9
Sheehan, Phil & Jean 63–4
shelter 15
shortness of breath 77
sibling relationships 68
sight 29, 108

silent intelligence 196–7
simplicity 144, 146
sinus problems 77
sleep 14, 23, 27
 deep 200
 environment for 212
 five R's 212–13
 functions 23–4, 210–11
 preparing for 211–12
 quality of 211
 quality sleep 210–13
smell (sense of) 29, 30, 108
smoking 24, 123–6
 limiting patterns 130–7
smoking cessation 107
 case studies 124, 126, 133–4, 135–6
 questions to ask 140
 roadblocks 98–9, 131–3
 weight gain 96–7, 131
socialisation 15
sore throat 77
soul 33, 45
spirit 33, 34, 45
spiritual balance 210, 216
spiritual energy 23, 32–4
spiritual goals 92, 102
spirituality 32
stability 147
Strecher, Dr Vic 131, 132
stress 19, 23, 71–5
 and addiction 132
 awareness of 75–6
 case studies 71–5
 defined 3–4
 internalised 120
 medical treatment 81–2, 86–7
 and meditation 199–200
 physical signs/symptoms 76–82, 86, 122–3

psychological signs/symptoms
82–3, 86, 120–2
reasons for 17, 180
relief from 32
see also acute stress
stress management 24
subconscious mind 95, 107, 108,
139, 152, 215
success 205
suicide 66, 85
superego 194
supra-ventricular tachycardia 62
survival 14, 15, 35, 37, 38
of the fittest 183
Sybil 122
sympathetic nervous system
13–14, 15
symptoms, as escape hatch 112,
120

taste 29, 30–1, 108
teenagers 68, 195
television viewing 100, 191, 214
temporal lobe epilepsy 56
temporal lobes, of brain 113
tension headaches 122
terrorism 19–20, 202
Terry (case study) 181
testosterone 119, 183
Think and Grow Rich (Hill) 205
thinking 197
creative 188, 215
de Bono's six thinking hats
160
defective 9
lateral 97–8
left-brain 214
right-brain 215
thinking-feeling connection
206–8

Thomas, Reverend Lionel 151,
155
thoughts, writing down 152, 153
thrill-seeking 16, 37
time 192
time away 161, 179
time management 157–62
time-wasting 100–1, 159–60
Tolle, Eckhart 189
touch 29, 31–2, 108
training 105
transcendental meditation 198–9
Travers, Bill 38
Trent and Diane (case study)
172–3, 174
twin studies 65

uncertainty 111
universal energy 23

value adding 19
valuing a partner 186–7
Violet (elderly patient) 48
viral illness 86
vision *see* sight
visualisation 95, 107–9, 143
dealing with stress 153
making changes 207–8
voice
hoarse 77
varying intensity 77

Watkins, George 208–9
weight gain, after smoking
cessation 96–7, 131
weight, ideal 92
weight loss 93–4, 141
Whiteley, Brett 208, 209
will (desire) 205
Wilson, Robert 117–18

work   23, 24, 26, 192   writing   107, 206
  inefficiency   159
  overwork   72, 101   youth   45, 66
worry   83
woundology (Myss)   49, 185   Zemanek, Stan   3, 4